FMCG Selling

T0194593

Leo Gough

- Fast-track route to mastering the sophisticated and highly competitive world of FMCG selling

- Covers the key issues of retailer dominance, retailer resistance to new product launches, consumer behavior, category management, buying structures, product development and regulation, and branding issues

- Case material from Proctor & Gamble, Coca-Cola and Pepsi, Wal-Mart and Red Bull

- Includes a comprehensive resources guide, key concepts and thinkers, a 10-step action plan, and a section of FAQs

SALES
12.08

Copyright © Capstone Publishing, 2003

The right of Leo Gough to be identified as the author of this book has been asserted in accordance with the Copyright, Designs and Patents Act 1988

First Published 2003 by
Capstone Publishing Limited (a Wiley company)
8 Newtec Place
Magdalen Road
Oxford OX4 1RE
United Kingdom
http://www.capstoneideas.com

CIP catalogue records for this book are available from the British Library and the US Library of Congress

ISBN 1-84112-461-3

Wiley also publishes its books in a variety of electronic formats. Some content that appears in print may not be available in electronic books.

Websites often change their contents and addresses; details of sites listed in this book were accurate at the time of writing, but may change.

Contents

Introduction to ExpressExec

ExpressExec is a completely up-to-date resource of current business practice, accessible in a number of ways – anytime, anyplace, anywhere. ExpressExec combines best practice cases, key ideas, action points, glossaries, further reading, and resources.

Each module contains 10 individual titles that cover all the key aspects of global business practice. Written by leading experts in their field, the knowledge imparted provides executives with the tools and skills to increase their personal and business effectiveness, benefiting both employee and employer.

ExpressExec is available in a number of formats:

» **Print** – 120 titles available through retailers or printed on demand using any combination of the 1200 chapters available.
» **E-Books** – e-books can be individually downloaded from ExpressExec.com or online retailers onto PCs, handheld computers, and e-readers.
» **Online** – http://www.expressexec.wiley.com/ provides fully searchable access to the complete ExpressExec resource via the Internet – a cost-effective online tool to increase business expertise across a whole organization.

» **ExpressExec Performance Support Solution (EEPSS)** – a software solution that integrates ExpressExec content with interactive tools to provide organizations with a complete internal management development solution.

» **ExpressExec Rights and Syndication** – ExpressExec content can be licensed for translation or display within intranets or on Internet sites.

To find out more visit www.ExpressExec.com or contact elound@wiley-capstone.co.uk.

Introduction to FMCG Selling

- » The changing nature of FMCG.
- » The rise of retailer power.
- » The selling wars – a zero-sum game?

Marketing fast-moving consumer goods (FMCG) is one of the "purest" and most sophisticated forms of selling there is. The great FMCG-selling companies, such as Procter & Gamble and Coca-Cola, invented mass marketing almost single-handedly and grew to become multinational giants in the process. FMCG played a major role in the rise of consumerism during the twentieth century and drove the development of the media from the days of the sponsored radio show of the 1920s. Selling FMCG provided the funds for the mushrooming growth of television and the establishment of advertising agencies as a vast, lucrative industry. In the West, and now increasingly in the rest of the world, almost everyone's lives are touched by FMCG.

Definitions of FMCG vary, but generally the term is used to mean branded products that are:

» used at least once a month;
» used directly by the end-consumer;
» non-durable; and
» sold in packaged form.

The main FMCG segments are:

» personal care – toothpaste, hair-care, skincare, soap, cosmetics, and paper products such as tissues and sanitary towels;
» household care – fabric wash (laundry soaps and synthetic detergents) and household cleaners (such as dish/utensil cleaners, air-fresheners and insecticides);
» branded and packaged food and beverages – soft drinks, cereals, biscuits, snack food, chocolates, ice cream, tea, coffee, vegetables, meat, bottled water, etc.; and
» spirits and tobacco.

It's not hard to see just how deeply they penetrate our domestic lives. In the "post-modern" West, attitudes towards FMCG are changing along with consumer behavior, and numerous lobby groups pressurize large corporations as part of a general attempt to foster many kinds of social reform. FMCG firms are easy targets of consumer boycotts, and must pay closer attention to notions of corporate responsibility than ever before. "Green" issues, health issues, and fears about biotechnology are just a few matters that companies cannot afford to ignore. In much of the developing world, however, FMCG are still welcomed as a symbol of progress towards prosperity. Many people in Russia and China, for instance, want as much FMCG as they can get. For leading brand manufacturers, the real opportunities for growth lie in these newer markets.

In the West, power has shifted from the manufacturers to the retailers, and competition has intensified. It's often a bitter struggle, as salespeople for supermarket suppliers battle for space on the shelves and are trapped in a cycle of wasteful trade promotions that they cannot control. Retailers are consolidating, but are only just beginning to step outside their home territories. If they are successful, it is likely to drive down manufacturers' prices, hurting brand equity.

The leading FMCG brands sell at a hefty premium, but with the greater power of the retailers, and the introduction of their own "private label" brands, second-tier brands are losing out and smaller manufacturers may go out of business. It's a secretive, highly complex war, where too many products are vying for customers' money. Many selling tactics are only successful for a short while, as competitors strangle one another in what in many respects is a zero-sum game.

For the salesperson in the field, it can be difficult to get a coherent overview of what is really happening. Selling into stores has little to do with personal selling skills, and is focused on getting a small edge in an endless, probably unwinnable, war. That small edge, however, can translate into hefty profits – for a while.

This book aims to give a picture of how products are sold in this dynamic and ever-changing industry.

What is Meant by FMCG Selling?

» Category management.
» Category captains.
» Slotting allowances and other payments.
» Do slotting allowances lead to better-selling products?

In the consumer goods markets of the US and Europe, a major structural change has occurred during the last two decades. Power has shifted from the manufacturers and wholesalers to a small group of large retailers. The middlemen – wholesalers and brokers – are being driven out of business altogether. In the US, for example, the number of grocery wholesalers declined from 400 in 1981 to 10 in 1998. Traditional supermarket operators, as well as general merchandisers such as Wal-Mart, have developed "supercenters" where both food and general goods are sold, sharing the same checkout counters. Roughly one-third of a typical US supercenter is devoted to supermarket-type goods, which are offered at competitive prices in the hope of increasing the number of customers who then "cross over" to purchase general goods at higher profit margins. In the US, relatively large manufacturers are now quite dependent on a few large retailers for their sales. Wal-Mart, for instance, is a major customer of Rubber Maid (15%), Fruit of the Loom (16%), and Toastmaster (30%).

The dominant retailers practice "power-buying," a collection of methods designed to reduce costs and increase buying power as much as possible. These include:

» category management, which uses IT to generate timely, accurate data to help maximize the profit potential in each product category as a whole; and
» "listing fees," also called "slotting allowances," which manufacturers pay on an annual basis to guarantee places on the shelves for their goods.

CATEGORY MANAGEMENT

Retailers use "category management" to analyze demand within a particular product category, such as toothpaste, to allocate shelf space between different products, and to make marketing plans for the category. Although it has been used by many retailers for years, supermarkets have only recently adopted the approach.

In category management, all decisions about product selection, placement, promotion, and pricing are made on a category-by-category basis, almost as if the category were a separate business. By consolidating these tasks, retailers believe that they make good efficiency gains and maximize their profit potential.

Unlike the slotting allowance system (see below), category management actively chooses which products to stock. Some retailers use both approaches, for example by selecting new products on a category management basis and then charging slotting allowances, while others use either method depending on the circumstances.

Category captains

A "category captain" is an outside firm, usually a major supplier, which advises retailers on how to manage a category. Manufacturers are generally more knowledgeable about their product groups than even the largest retailer, with detailed, up-to-date knowledge of matters such as the times of year when a product will sell best, the most effective promotions, and what kind of products should be displayed nearby.

The role of the category captain varies widely. Some retailers don't use them at all; others obtain advice but then compare it with the opinions of other suppliers and their own data; while others allow category captains to manage categories entirely, especially in marginal lines such as magazines.

There are concerns that category captains can abuse their position in various ways. For example, a category captain can acquire commercially sensitive information about other suppliers' plans and use it against them. In order to advise effectively, the captain needs to see its competitors' plans in advance for key areas such as promotion, new products, and advertising campaigns, giving it an incentive to devise counter-plans or to decide not to compete in a certain area.

There may also be a temptation to give retailers misleading advice in order to thwart rivals. A captain who influences product placement could advise the retailer to put its major rivals' products in disadvantageous locations or recommend it not to carry a competing product at all. This might not affect the category's performance from the retailer's perspective, but smaller manufacturers are acutely sensitive to the problem, often arguing that not only are they sometimes allocated poor or insufficient shelf space but are also often excluded altogether. Retailers tend to deny that this occurs, or say that a captain who gives poor advice is likely to be phased out.

A category captain who works for competing retailers is in a position to form a kind of cartel by giving the same advice to all its clients, which would tend to fix prices and product placement. It can do the same with leading manufacturers, although retailers are likely to resist such an attempt. According to food consultant Robert L. Steiner, some category captains (leading manufacturing firms in their fields) visit retailers to urge them to raise the price of their private labels in line with a planned price hike of a leading brand, in order to maintain the price difference at the same level. Using commissioned research from a market research firm, the category captains said that this would be more profitable for retailers than attempting to increase market share by not changing the prices of the private labels or only increasing them slightly. Steiner regards this as an effort "to prevent their customers' private labels from using the price weapon against them" and, in his view, these leading brand manufacturers "considered the private labels to be close competitors, e.g., to be in the same relevant product market."

SLOTTING ALLOWANCES AND OTHER PAYMENTS

You're working for a small manufacturer that has developed a great new soft drink, and you are asked to approach a supermarket chain to see if they will take it on. They're interested, but they require a payment per store to make room for your product on the shelves – the charge will run into many thousands of pounds. A simple case of extortion? Not in the supermarket business, where this type of fee, known as a "slotting allowance" is common practice.

According to research by Gregory T. Gundlach, associate professor of marketing at the University of Notre Dame, retailers defend slotting allowances for new products on the grounds that it offsets some of the cost and risk of adopting a new product line. Suppliers, on the other hand, tend to think that the fee is far higher than the store's costs and is simply a way of making more money.

Retailers usually express the slotting allowance as a fee per "stock-keeping unit" (SKU) per store. In the US charges are thought to range from $75 to $300 per SKU per store, with the cost of slotting a new product nationwide exceeding $4mn. Manufacturers often wish to sell more than one item – for example, several flavours of a soft drink – so the cost of introducing a modest range of four new products could cost more than $16mn.

What's more, you, the manufacturer, must pay these charges as a lump sum in advance, but the retailer makes no guarantee to buy a specific amount of your goods, or even to buy at all after the expiry of a trial period (which may be six months or less).

Slotting allowances are a one-off charge, but the supplier's difficulties do not end there. Many retailers also charge a "pay-to-stay" fee, in advance, to keep your product on the shelves for a given period, usually a year. This is often justified as an auction of limited shelf space – the "new product risk" argument does not apply.

Retailers certainly do face increased costs with problem products – restocking, re-tagging, changing inventory software, and the opportunity cost of lost sales add up to a substantial expense. However, major manufacturers such as Procter & Gamble simply refuse to pay any fees or allowances at all, yet are able to get their products into the stores. Not all retailers approve of the practice either. Wal-Mart, for instance, makes no charges, preferring to use category management instead, and signs contracts with its suppliers that are intended to create good long-term relationships.

Another fee charged by some retailers is to secure exclusivity – in other words, to keep competitors' products off the shelves or relegate them to a worse position in the store. Smaller manufacturers (of products such as tinned tomatoes, tortillas, and air-fresheners in the US) have complained that market leaders in their industry make such payments for the sole purpose of keeping the smaller competitors out.

Even if your products are not excluded altogether, poor positioning is likely to damage sales. Although competition law regulators are researching the problem, many suppliers are unwilling to make open complaints against their customers, especially because if several of them joined to sue a retailer, a supplier who stayed out of the battle would probably get more business.

Do slotting allowances lead to better-selling products?

Ideally, a store decides which items to stock based on what it thinks will sell the best – and at the lower-margin end of the business, this is especially crucial. Supporters of slotting allowances sometimes argue that the fees are a way of screening new products – the idea being that a manufacturer will only pay a price for shelf space for goods that it is certain will sell well. Since slotting fees are thought to account for around 16% of the cost of a new product introduction, they certainly *ought* to have such an effect, but neither manufacturers nor retailers see slotting fees as a good predictor of product sales, although they agree that the fees do result in higher retail prices.

KEY LEARNING POINTS

» In the last few years, power has shifted from the manufacturers of FMCG to the retailers, who use "power buying" and their own "private label" brands to maximize their own profits at the expense of their suppliers.

» "Category management" seeks to optimize sales within a product category by treating each product category as if it were a stand-alone business.

» Stores often appoint a major supplier as the "category captain" to advise on the best product mix within a category. Arrangements vary, from simple advice-giving to a large degree of autonomy for the category captain. There are fears that some category captains may use their position to damage competitors or to create cartels.

» Many retailers charge fees to manufacturers for the right to place their products on their shelves, such as slotting allowances, "pay-to-stay" fees, and exclusivity fees. Some major manufacturers have enough bargaining power to refuse to pay such fees, but many small suppliers claim to be squeezed out of the market by these fees.

» The definition of a "stock-keeping unit" (SKU) is narrow, and different flavors of the same product are considered to be different SKUs. Since retailers charge slotting fees per SKU, slotting fees are often multiplied.

» Slotting allowances do not, according to both manufacturers and retailers, lead to better-selling products.

The Evolution of FMCG Selling

» Procter & Gamble – the great innovator.
» The invention of brand management.
» The advent of market research.
» Going global.
» The decline in innovation.
» Coca-Cola.
» The 1980s – brand equity.
» The 1990s – brands in crisis?
» The brand backlash.
» Consumer boycotts.
» Time-line.

The origins of FMCG lie in the nineteenth century, when better transportation allowed commodities to be moved rapidly from their point of origin. In the US in particular, where huge distances and a rapidly expanding population provided enormous opportunities for business, manufacturers began to give brand names to their goods. Initially, brands were simply a kind of quality assurance – customers learned that "Brand X" was of better, or more consistent, quality than the generic product – but gradually firms began to find ways to make their brands more valuable. In this chapter we will look at two firms that played a central role in developing FMCG marketing from the nineteenth century until today: Procter & Gamble and Coca-Cola.

PROCTER & GAMBLE – THE GREAT INNOVATOR

In 1837 William Procter, a candle-maker, and James Gamble, a soap-maker, combined their businesses in Cincinnati, founding what was to become arguably the most inventive consumer goods firm of all time, the bellwether of the FMCG industries.

"P&G," as it is often known, prospered during the Civil War through lucrative military contracts. Railroads spread rapidly after the Civil War, allowing firms such as P&G to market their goods across the country. Improved postal services and better printing eventually led to a boom in magazines, particularly women's magazines, such as the *Ladies' Home Journal* and *The Homemaker*, carrying advertising for branded packaged goods.

In the 1880s, P&G took the then unheard-of step of advertising its Ivory soap brand direct to consumers across the whole country, and in 1896 it took out its first color print advertisement, which was for Ivory in *Cosmopolitan* magazine. Within a few years it was selling more than 30 kinds of soap products. With the advent of electricity, the candle-making business slowed, and was finally discontinued in the 1920s, but soap was still big business, and remains one of P&G's most important products today.

Astonishingly, P&G remained a partnership until 1890, when it finally became a corporation. It established one of the first profit-sharing schemes and was among the first companies to create its own research and development unit, a lab at Ivorydale that worked to improve its soap-manufacturing. Among the lab's early R&D triumphs were: Ivory Flakes, a soap in flake form for washing clothes and dishes; Chipso, the first soap designed for washing machines; Dreft, the first household synthetic detergent; and, in 1911, Crisco, the first branded vegetable cooking oil.

The invention of brand management

In 1931 a P&G employee, Neil McElroy, circulated a memo calling for specialized teams to work exclusively on specific brands, treating them as if they were stand-alone businesses. McElroy had been working on a campaign for Camay soap and had become frustrated with apparent conflicts with P&G's main soap brand, Ivory. He proposed targeting different brands, such as Camay and Ivory, at different markets, and working to distinguish their different qualities – what is now called "product differentiation."

McElroy's suggestions were adopted enthusiastically by the firm and he eventually became its CEO, with a now-familiar motto of: "Find out what the consumers want and give it to them." The technique of brand management – balancing centralized supervision with the devolution of decision-making to brand managers – was widely copied and became one of the defining features of American marketing.

The advent of market research

In 1925, P&G formed a market research department. It took extreme pains to learn how its customers used its products, employing hundreds of housewives to test its cleaning and cooking goods and report on their experiences. Teams of researchers were sent out to interview women all across America about cooking, laundry, dishwashing, and so on, with strict instructions not to carry forms with them. Researchers were expected to have excellent memories – after an informal talk with the consumer, the researcher would rush back to the car to write detailed notes.

The purpose was to discover as much as possible about how consumers used products made by P&G and its competitors, and how the products might be improved. Much attention was paid to the effectiveness of advertising, and the firm is said to have known more about audience sizes than the radio stations themselves. It was the heyday of radio and the P&G cooking oil brand, Crisco, began to sponsor cooking shows that reached millions of women across the country. With the coming of television in America in the 1950s, the firm pioneered the TV soap opera with great success.

By the 1960s, cheaper telephone calls dramatically cut the costs of market research by making telephone market surveys possible, and the door-to-door researcher was phased out. Focus groups and other statistically significant sampling methods were introduced.

Going global

By 1945, P&G was worth nearly $350mn and was selling in Canada and the UK as well as in the US. In 1946 it introduced a new soap powder, Tide, which was superior to other products and became the engine for global expansion and new product development. A new toothpaste, Crest, achieved a coup by persuading the American Dental Association to endorse it, and in 1961 P&G invented disposable baby nappies, introducing Pampers. Since the end of World War II, P&G has continued to expand internationally, reaching 23 countries by 1980. During the 1980s, the firm expanded into healthcare products and cosmetics, purchasing major brands such as Max Factor. By 2000, it was selling its products in more than 70 countries, with subsidiaries in 70 of them, and reaching an estimated five billion consumers.

The decline in innovation

According to Durk Jager, P&G's current CEO, the firm's last really new innovation appeared in 1982, when it introduced Always, a sanitary towel with "wings" that attach firmly to underwear. Like other major brand manufacturers, P&G is under price pressure from competitors and the increased power of retailers. Market share is declining and the corporate culture has become risk-averse. Despite some notable recent successes, such as Sunny Delight, an orange-flavored drink, the unnerving fact is that innovation doesn't seem to pay – industry-wide, an estimated 70% of new products fail in their first year, and there is widespread resistance from business people to accept new products.

Jager has been on an efficiency drive, firing staff, introducing performance measures that are linked to brands rather than to countries, closing factories, and shifting power from country managers to seven global business units (GBUs) organized by product category. He hopes to drastically reduce the time it takes to get a product to market, and to increase the number of genuinely new, hard-to-copy, product innovations. Time will reveal whether these measures will be enough, but P&G's heyday as the quintessential FMCG company – and virtual inventor of the consumer society – seems to be over.

COCA-COLA

In the 1880s there were many companies selling carbonated soft drinks in the US, both through soda fountains and in bottles. There were few barriers to entry – it was inexpensive to set up a bottling plant and there was no patent protection for proprietary flavors.

In 1886 John Pemberton, a pharmacist, invented a medicinal drink that he called Coca-Cola. Marketed as an "Ideal Brain Tonic and Sovereign Remedy for Headache and Nervousness," it was sold at drug-store soda fountains. In 1889, Benjamin Thomas and Joseph Whitehead persuaded the firm to give them the exclusive right, in perpetuity, to bottle and market Coca-Cola throughout most of the US. The company was reluctant to get into the bottling business itself, but also worried that a third-party bottler might produce a poor quality product. White-head and Thomas convinced the company that they would meet its quality conditions, and obtained the rights for the nominal sum of $1. Coca-Cola kept all rights to the soda fountain business.

Whitehead and Thomas quickly sold off a number of licenses (again, exclusive and in perpetuity) to regional bottlers in order to raise capital and Coca-Cola's great expansion began. Most of the sublicensed territories were purchased by family businesses and covered a small area due to the high cost of transportation (bottles were returnable). In 1891 Asa G. Candler, an entrepreneur from Atlanta, Georgia, obtained control of the business and displayed a remarkable flair in merchandising, establishing Coca-Cola nationwide.

By 1900 there were more than 100 brands of "soda pop" in the US, and more than 2500 bottling plants. Ginger ale was the most popular flavor, and the industry was booming. In 1904 Coca-Cola had more than 120 bottling plants. By 1919 there were 1200.

Asa Candler was a great marketing innovator. He began to reposition Coke as a revitalizing drink rather than as a medicinal tonic and broke new ground in the search for ways of creating intellectual property around the product. Everything that could be patented or trademarked, from the logo to the formula, was fiercely protected in court (the name "Coca-Cola" itself was registered in the US Patent Office in 1893). New advertising gimmicks, including the use of celebrities, were tried and the perpetual sublicenses that it had granted turned out to be an advantage – the firm's bottlers had a strong motive to join in the mass marketing effort.

By 1940 Coca-Cola dominated the US market with a share of about 50%. Newer competitors, such as Pepsi-Cola and 7UP, copied its methods and became major rivals. By 1960, these firms, along with Royal Crown, had 75% of the US market, and by 1980, having been joined by Dr Pepper, they had captured 80% of the carbonated soft drinks market, including private labels. Dr Pepper was a regional brand that was founded before Coca-Cola, and had benefited from a court ruling that Dr Pepper was not a cola, which allowed tied cola-bottlers to manufacture it.

THE 1980S – BRAND EQUITY

During the 1980s, a feeling began to emerge that many old-line companies were too fat for their own good. Financial liberalization made possible a wave of mergers, acquisitions, buy-outs, and spin-offs that were intended to take the power out of the hands of entrenched management and place it back with the true owners of the companies, the shareholders. There was also a lot of excitement about the potential for moving manufacturing facilities abroad, and a sense that the emphasis in business should not be on manufacturing *per se*, but on better marketing.

In 1988 the concept of "brand equity" became suddenly meaningful when Philip Morris acquired Kraft for $12.6bn, some $10bn of which was what accountants called "goodwill," but was, in essence, a payment for the corporate brand. In the heady financial boom of the late 1980s, it was important to be able to value such intangibles because there was a chance to trade in them on the stock market. The theory of branding as an abstract, yet tradable, notion had arrived and many organizations, including government departments, unwisely leaped on the brand bandwagon.

THE 1990S – BRANDS IN CRISIS?

The FMCG industry has been the primary innovator in the art and science of branding for at least half a century, but the method had been generally regarded as a way of strengthening a business in the long term, rather than creating a business asset that could be sold off quickly.

During the 1990s doubts began to emerge about the future of many FMCG brands. The key event was "Marlboro Friday," April 2, 1993, when Philip Morris suddenly cut the price of Marlboro cigarettes by 20% in an attempt to compete with bargain brands that were beginning to become serious rivals – in the previous nine months, generic cigarettes had increased their share of the US market from 28% to 36%, while Marlboro had 22%. The strategy worked – by December, Marlboro's share had risen to 27%, but at the cost of substantially lower profits.

On "Marlboro Friday," the share prices of all the major consumer brands fell sharply. Industry giants such as Heinz, Coca-Cola, PepsiCo, and P&G were all affected. Analysts thought that "brand equity," the goodwill value of brands, had crashed and theorized that consumers were now "brand blind" and did not want to pay the premiums for named brands – price was now king.

THE BRAND BACKLASH

Recently, a number of influential books have appeared attacking the whole system of branding consumer goods, such as Eric Schlosser's *Fast Food Nation* and *The World is Not for Sale* by François Dufour and José Bové. The most publicized is *No Logo: Taking Aim at the Brand Bullies* by Naomi Klein. According to Klein, brand equity has become so important to firms that their principal focus is on creating a kind of consumer dreamworld, "a Barbie world for adults," where the emphasis is on exploiting consumers' lifestyle aspirations as a way of selling them products that are now often produced by faceless third parties in the developing world.

Branding techniques have become so widespread, with governments and NGOs as concerned about their images as are the original FMCG manufacturers, that the whole concept of branding has been watered down – heavyweight movie mogul Michael Eisner calls the word "brand" "overused, sterile and unimaginative." Brands are losing their power as consumers become less loyal and manufacturing standards rise, making it harder for brand leaders to compete on quality alone. The values of 1950s America, when P&G could send researchers to discuss domestic chores with thousands of housewives across the nation, has gone forever. In the developed world, consumers are cynical, distracted and pushed for time. While consumers in newly-affluent countries such as Singapore still have a hunger for brands, Western customers seem far more concerned with trying to force brand-owning corporations into adopting "socially responsible" polices. The age of the consumer boycott is upon us.

CONSUMER BOYCOTTS

In 1880 Captain C.C. Boycott, an Irish land agent who tried to evict tenant farm-workers after they refused to accept a wage cut, was the subject of an organized resistance that gave rise to the term "boycott." People refused to work for Boycott, sell him goods, or even speak to him, and he eventually had to leave the country. A campaigner, James Redpath, advised boycotters that "if you see a land-grabber going to a shop to buy bread, or clothing, or even whiskey, go you to the shopkeeper at once, [and] say to him that under British law he has the undoubted right to sell his goods to anyone, but that there is no British law to compel you to buy another penny's worth from him, and that you will never do it as long as you live."

Consumer boycotts have had a long history, and many have been highly effective. Although today they tend to be associated with the political left, this has not always been the case, such as the Nazi-inspired boycotting of Jewish-owned shops in Germany during the 1930s. Southern Baptist Convention called for a boycott of Disney because of that company's position on homosexuality (such as its policy of extending health benefits to same-sex partners of employees). Here are a few other examples of successful consumer boycotts.

» **1766**: the New England colonials' boycott of British goods led to the repeal of the Stamp Act by the British government.
» **1940s**: Gandhi organized boycotts of British salt and cloth as part of the movement for Indian independence.

» **1955**: in the US, the Montgomery bus boycott, a protest against bus segregation, bankrupts the bus company and sparks off the civil rights movement.

» **1960s**: protesters against the Vietnam War organize a boycott of Saran Wrap, made by Dow Chemicals, because the firm also manufactured napalm. The company's image suffers for years.

» **1986**: Barclays Bank pulls out of South Africa following boycotts elsewhere by anti-apartheid protesters.

Today, consumer boycotts are widespread, and are having a major influence on corporate behavior, particularly on FMCG firms.

TIME-LINE

» **1800s**: manufacturers begin to brand their goods as a way of promising quality.

» **1880s**: in the US, P&G advertises Ivory soap nationally.

» **1886**: Coca-Cola invented.

» **1889**: Benjamin Thomas and Joseph Whitehead sell off regional Coca-Cola bottling rights to small firms around the US.

» **1890s**: P&G starts its R&D unit to look for product innovations.

» **1893**: Coca-Cola registered at US Patent Office.

» **1900**: there are 100 brands of carbonated soft drinks in the US. Ginger ale is the most popular flavor.

» **1920s**: P&G's Crisco cooking oil sponsors radio cookery shows.

» **1925**: P&G establishes its market research department, pioneering media audience analysis and consumer interviews.

» **1931**: Neil McElroy persuades P&G to run brands as if they were stand-alone businesses, and introduces the concept of brand differentiation.

» **1940s**: Gandhi organizes boycotts of British salt and cloth.

» **1946**: P&G launches Tide, which becomes its most important product.

» **1950s**: TV comes to the US, and P&G sponsors highly successful soap operas.

» **1955**: the Montgomery bus boycott establishes the civil rights movement.

» **1957**: a book, *The Hidden Persuaders*, by Vance Packard, attacks consumer marketing methods.
» **1960s**: P&G pioneers telephone market research and focus groups.
» **1963**: P&G launches Pampers, the first disposable nappy.
» **1988**: Philip Morris acquires Kraft, valuing its brand identity at around $10bn. "Brand equity" is born.
» **1993**: on "Marlboro Friday," April 2, Philip Morris suddenly slashes the price of Marlboro cigarettes by 20%, sparking off a severe fall in the share prices of leading brand manufacturers.

KEY LEARNING POINTS

» FMCG manufacturing has its origin in the nineteenth century and was very innovative in its approach to marketing. With a huge potential demand, key areas were developing better products and advertising widely. Brands were a form of quality assurance but were rarely protected in law.
» By the 1920s P&G was pioneering the scientific approach to market research, interviewing thousands of consumers. The commercially sponsored radio show appeared.
» In the 1930s, P&G invents brand management, treating its many soap products as if they were separate stand-alone businesses, targeted at different sectors of the market. In the homogeneous, conformist consumer markets of 1950s America, TV advertising and the soap opera are enormously powerful ways to sell FMCG.
» In the 1960s and 1970s, many FMCG marketing techniques travel abroad as the rest of the world becomes affluent enough to buy consumer goods.
» During the merger mania of the 1980s, brand equity becomes quantifiable when huge sums are paid for Kraft and other firms. Excitement about creating value by branding goes too far; the increase in affluent consumers across the world brings with it diversity of taste and attitudes, and they become less "brand loyal."

The E-Dimension

» Scanner marketing.
» The challenge of "data mining."
» Scanners – deathwish marketing?
» The individual store as a brand?
» Coming soon – RFID tags.
» Best practice – Wal-Mart.

So far, FMCG e-tailing has had relatively limited success and the real impact of the Internet has been behind the scenes in the supply chain. As a low-margin, high-volume business, FMCG selling has a particularly strong need for precise sales analysis and real-time information about product sales across thousands of stores. The Internet serves as a conduit for some of this information, and is part of an array of IT applications that are being used to gather sales data and make sense of them.

In this chapter we will look at how the FMCG industry is trying to get ever-more precise sales data, and how it attempts to use them. One major problem is how to use the information intelligently – data on their own can overwhelm you, and there is some evidence that many firms are not using this resource as effectively as they could.

SCANNER MARKETING

Before the advent of scanners, manufacturers relied upon store audit data, syndicated by firms like ACNielsen, and warehouse withdrawals data, syndicated by firms like SAMI. When scanners were first introduced into stores, the data they generated were intended to be used simply to measure market share and track consumer sales, as a more precise replacement of information that was already being collected.

The first checkout scanner was installed in America at a Marsh Supermarket store on a trial basis in Troy, Ohio, in 1974. Food stores were the first to use scanners extensively. Retailers say that scanner technology has several advantages, such as improved checkout productivity, lower labor costs, and improved sales and inventory records that lead to more efficient space allocation and reordering. Simply not having to put prices on each product by hand saves an estimated $154,000 a year at the average supermarket, as well as reducing pricing errors – checkout cashiers who inputted prices manually made errors of 16%.

Retailers, manufacturers, and data companies have worked together to improve the reliability and accuracy of scanner data, leading to greater confidence in the quality of the data. They now use IT to discover instantly what they are selling in each of hundreds of stores, how much money they are making on each sale, and who their customers are. Checkout scanners and other advances in technology have allowed retailers to avoid carrying unnecessary stock and running out of goods that are in demand.

The result is that the industry is becoming more ambitious in how it uses scanner data – for example, to validate coupons by scanning, to reorder based on scans rather than physical stock-checks, and to help make decisions on promotions and product mixes within categories.

A major innovation occurred when Wal-Mart opened its information system to its suppliers and forced them to start using scanner data for these purposes. Prior to that, retailers tended to provide only sample data. By the mid-1990s, however, scanner data on about 70% of supermarket goods was being provided to the data companies who help manage the inter-company systems. Giving suppliers access to store-level information has generated a massive amount of new information which it is hoped will improve efficiency in marketing.

It has certainly given rise to a new marketing art, "scanner marketing" and the "Efficient Consumer Response" initiative (see Chapter 6), which aims to establish a system that is driven by consumer wants rather than by uncoordinated decisions along the supply chain.

For manufacturing companies, the data:

» provide more accurate monitoring of product sales as well as competitors' sales;
» helps firms to evaluate new products and the effectiveness of promotions and advertising;
» provides useful marketing information at the category and brand levels;
» enables more accurate sales forecasting; and
» helps firms to spot strategic marketing opportunities.

For retailers, the benefits include:

» improving the product mix within categories;
» maximizing shelf profitability;
» quick evaluation of new product performance; and
» better stock control.

A major problem is that the amount of data generated is very large and hard to analyze.

THE CHALLENGE OF "DATA MINING"

"Data mining" means the process of searching through very large amounts of data to find useful information. It's a paradise for statisticians, but can easily mislead non-mathematically inclined managers.

The task of finding real patterns in an ocean of data is formidable. For instance, suppose you are trying to discover whether your profit margins vary according to a pattern. You look at the figures and see that profits tend to increase in the autumn – should you conclude that there is a predictable seasonal variation? Not necessarily. Other factors may be varying also, such as sales volume and price discounts. If prices are lower in the summer but increase in the autumn, the increase in price in the autumn may be due to the price change – and by adjusting the figures to remove the effects of discounts you would discover this.

Used expertly, data mining can uncover hidden relationships, but there are many potential fallacies, often due to oversimplification. For example, a common way of deciding which products to stock within a category is to use "brand ranking." In brand ranking, each SKU within the category is listed according to various measures, such as sales, revenue, and volume, over a fixed time period such as three months. A retailer can simply look at the lists and throw out the weakest performer. At the level of the individual store, this method, while rough, might not be too damaging, but when considering many stores, it is likely to be a very poor decision.

Suppose the category is mustard. There are a wide variety of flavors, such as Dijon, English, and American, appealing to different types of consumer, and there are different kinds of container. People in richer parts of town might buy more Dijon and other foreign types, while people in poorer parts of town might prefer "traditional" brands. Brand ranking across many stores ignores these nuances and is likely to lead to gross overstocking of the wrong products in some stores.

The problem intensifies if you are ranking across many retail chains to try to get a picture of the whole market. In this case, the products are probably not equally available to be ranked, since one chain may stock far more products in a category than others. Ranking is so crude that potentially successful products that are only stocked by innovative retailers may be ignored or dropped.

SCANNERS – "DEATHWISH MARKETING"?

The term "deathwish marketing" was introduced in a 1991 book, *The Marketing Revolution*, by Kevin J. Clancy & Robert S. Shulman (HarperBusiness), to describe how brand managers can sometimes destroy a product by applying marketing methods inappropriately.

Professor John M. McCann of Fuqua School of Business, Duke University, argues that many managers have misused the sales data generated by scanning products at the checkout. In his view, the complex underlying data are often oversimplified – managers tend to pick out trends that are easy to understand and ignore other significant information. Specifically, McCann thinks that sales report graphs showing sales volume and prices over time have led to serious mistakes. On such a graph, large increases in sales volume during promotions (when there are price cuts) show up very obviously. Managers are tempted to try to sustain these volume increases for longer by increasing the number of promotions during the year.

But if your product category is not growing, increasing the number of promotions (or the promotion price cut) can be dangerous in the longer term. Says McCann, if, as consumers, we see that certain products are frequently sold at a discount "we begin to wonder why we ever paid full price for the item." Knowing that the product will frequently be on sale at a discount may lead shoppers only to buy during promotions, since they do not have long to wait. By increasing the number of promotions, managers have, in effect, simply made a permanent price cut.

McCann views the general increase in the number of product promotions as damaging overall, since it encourages consumers to lose their brand loyalty – they switch from brand to brand according to which one happens to be cheapest at the time. Market share can be increased in the short term at the expense of long-term brand equity.

THE INDIVIDUAL STORE AS A BRAND?

In the past, the focus tended to be away from the store, on areas such as:

» the manufacturer's operations;
» orders from retailers;

» delivery and dispatch at warehouses;
» how the manufacturer's sales force communicated with retail headquarters;
» how the retail headquarters made decisions; and
» how chains behaved as a group.

Although these focal points are all relevant, none of them is as central to marketing as what actually happens at each individual retail outlet. Until the advent of scanner marketing, however, firms were simply unable to measure what was happening in individual stores.

Although manufacturers' salespeople go into stores, it has generally been either to conduct a store check, where they record a "snapshot" of what happens to be in the store at that moment, or to write down what shelf space has been allocated to their own brands and those of their competitors. The retail outlet is where the customer encounters the product, and is clearly the most important point in the selling process. Every part of the marketing effort is devoted to encouraging shoppers to notice and purchase your product.

So, were manufacturers concentrating their efforts in the wrong place? Possibly – by trying hard to persuade retailers' central buying offices to accept its products and promotions, they may have contributed to the buyer's power. With the new, store-level data, manufacturers are now able to refine their marketing efforts to suit specific stores. To understand why this matters, think about a supermarket chain from the consumer's point of view.

As a consumer, you probably only go regularly to one outlet of any given chain – and it is that outlet that represents the chain to you. You get to know it intimately, and are likely to respond quickly to any changes, whether you perceive them as positive or negative. In this sense, the main store where you shop is very like a branded product that you buy regularly. UK retailer Marks & Spencer, for instance, has a flagship outlet at Marble Arch in London that stocks a far wider range of goods than most other stores, and is well-known to loyal customers across the country.

Regular customers can be identified through check and credit card purchases, and their behavior analyzed. Loyalty programs, customer feedback books, coupon mailings are just a few of the ways that a local store can target its regular customers.

COMING SOON – RFID TAGS

A new technology looks set to generate even more precise marketing data – radio frequency identification or RFID. RFID uses small memory chips ("tags") with a tiny radio antenna to transmit data about the object to which it is attached.

Wal-Mart is investing heavily in RFID tags in the hope of even greater efficiencies in supply-chain management, inventory, and theft prevention, as well as generating an even more real-time flow of data about the products on the shelves. Tests have examined how products travel through a store, and Wal-Mart is now trying out RFID tags on goods moving through the whole supply chain, all the way from the manufacturer to the checkout.

Currently, there are the following three types of tag.

» "Active" tags, powered by batteries, transmit a signal constantly. The obvious application is in situations where an electronic reader can't get close to an item, such as at a motorway toll station or a car park entrance.
» "Semi-passive" tags, also battery powered, only transmit when they receive a signal, which conserves battery energy.
» "Passive" tags, the cheapest type, have no battery at all, but can transmit data when they are close to a reader (currently the maximum effective distance is four feet). Passive tags are seen as the most appropriate for in-store applications.

There are still some technical problems. Environments where there are a lot of radio signals, such as factories and warehouses, confuse the tags, and they cannot receive or transmit through metal or – with some frequencies – through water. And they're still expensive, costing up to $2 each, which currently makes them uneconomic for using on small-value individual product items.

An alliance between a Californian chip manufacturer, Alien Technology, and Rafsec, a firm from Finland that will make the antennae, aims to bring prices for the tags down to as little as $0.15 by the end of 2003, and to cut that figure by two-thirds in 2005. At that price level, RFID suddenly becomes very interesting indeed, although it will still require a heavy investment, not only in the tags themselves but also in the hardware and software needed to read, store, and transmit all the information.

This opens up some attractive possibilities for after-sales marketing. For example, a package could transmit information about whether food or medicine had passed its sell-by date to a monitor in the kitchen or to your home computer. Meanwhile, shelves in a supermarket could "tell" the stockroom that they are getting empty.

BEST PRACTICE – WAL-MART

Retail giant Wal-Mart has more than 10,000 suppliers, which presents an enormous challenge as it tries to fulfill its promise of ensuring that customers can always obtain the products they need at "everyday low prices" – which means, among other things, correctly estimating fluctuating demand. It is the biggest private-sector employer in the world, with 1.2 million employees, and is now the biggest grocery retailer in the US, although it only entered the food business in the mid-1990s.

For many years, the company has been a leading innovator in using IT to co-ordinate the process of getting the right product mix onto the right shelves – its main computer is claimed to be the most powerful in the world, after the Pentagon's.

The most important system that Wal-Mart runs is Retail Link, an interface between the firm and its manufacturers, which allows suppliers to:

» download purchase orders from Wal-Mart;
» check the status of their invoices to Wal-Mart;
» find out how many of their products were sold at Wal-Mart outlets on the previous day and analyze the effects of price cuts and returns on store inventory;
» see reports on sales of their products going back as far as two years;
» see sales forecasts for their products for up to one year; and
» input information into Wal-Mart's system.

All suppliers have full access to information relating to their own products, while some also receive, at Wal-Mart's discretion, information about competing brands.

Wal-Mart uses EDI (Electronic Data Interchange) to process invoices and purchase orders. About two-thirds of its suppliers use EDI to accept purchase orders, while about one-third send their invoices via EDI – but in fact this covers the vast majority of the billing paperwork (85% of invoices and 93% of purchase orders). The system streamlines the delivery process and keeps stockholding low.

Retail Link has been accessible to approved suppliers via the Internet since 1997, and is processed through Wal-Mart's data warehouse, which stores an astonishing 100 terabytes of information. Information is gathered on the day's trading until midnight, and is available on the system by 4.00 a.m. the next morning. A major aim is to ensure that individual stores get the right stock, in the right volume, for *their* customers.

While Wal-Mart does not release personal information about individual customers to its suppliers, it does give them very detailed information about store-level transactions. One such area is "item affinity." If many customers buy, say, skin cream and shampoo on the same shopping trip, Wal-Mart moves the items closer together in that particular store. With some other buying patterns, for example if customers tend to buy two of an item at the same time, Wal-Mart makes a suggestion through Retail Link – in this case that the supplier produces twin packs.

Until recently, Wal-Mart, like other large retailers, also supplied some of its data to market research firms such as ACNielsen and Information Resources, who sell sales information gleaned from the industry as a whole. Research firms sell this aggregated information to manufacturers and retailers who are looking for the bigger picture. Many in the industry are known to compare trends derived from Wal-Mart's Retail Link system with this third-party "syndicated" data.

The "bump" and poor data

The syndicated sales figures industry-wide do not tally with manufacturers' delivery records. Many believe that the explanation for this "bump" in sales reporting is due to some retailers inflating sales figures in order to obtain larger cash payments from their suppliers (relating to volume discounts).

Wal-Mart has a reputation as a fair dealer with its suppliers, and is thought not to indulge in such practices. While no one has criticized the quality of Wal-Mart's own data, there have been complaints that some of the aggregated industry data may be incorrect.

In July 2002, Wal-Mart announced that it would no longer supply its information to the research firms. The company denies that this has anything to do with inaccuracies in the aggregated data, and suggests that it is because Wal-Mart, as the biggest player in the market, is giving away more than it receives by providing information to the whole industry.

The decision will not affect its own suppliers, who will continue to use Retail Link as before. Industry commentators say that this is part of a trend for progressive retailers to become even more involved with targeted marketing at the level of individual stores. Wal-Mart's aim, it seems, is not to hurt manufacturers, but to maintain its competitive edge over competing retailers who do not have such sophisticated systems for data mining.

KEY LEARNING POINTS

» Scanner data is the marketer's dream, offering the potential for pinpoint accuracy in the study of how individual consumers behave in stores, as well as allowing those retailers who have stable relationships with their suppliers to make the whole process of matching supply to demand much more efficient.

» The quantity of data that scanners generate is mind-boggling. Wal-Mart is the leader in its analysis and has pioneered the sharing of this information with its suppliers, who can access it from a home computer via the Internet.

» Industry-wide sharing of data is more problematic, and Wal-Mart recently cancelled its contracts with the market research firms who collate the data. The problem with this kind of co-operation between rivals is that some participants may be tempted to "cheat," which makes the data less accurate. Detailed sales information is very valuable to competitors, so it is unlikely that co-operative systems can ever be as good as the largest in-house data warehouses.

» Many managers are not properly trained in how to use the data, and make elementary mistakes in interpretation (such as the brand-ranking system). While larger firms employ statistical experts to analyze the data, their interpretations are not always communicated well to other decision-makers, who have easy access to standard software report features that are potentially misleading.

The Global Dimension

» Western consolidation in retail.
» Is the Euro deflationary for FMCG?
» Lookalike products – attacking brands.
» Best practice – private labels versus leading brands.

Although leading brand manufacturers are among the most internationalized of firms, the push for globalization came late to the supermarket industry and is still at a relatively early stage.

For some years food retailers have been consolidating in the US and western Europe, leading to the emergence – in the US, UK, France, and Germany – of big players with global ambitions. The main factors driving this consolidation are:

» cheaper transactions arising from advances in IT;
» a general trend in the US away from regional to nationwide businesses;
» the continuing effort towards greater economic integration within the EU, including the abolition of internal tariffs and the introduction of a single currency, the Euro;
» growth in car ownership, making large, edge-of-town superstores possible;
» greater economies of scale due to technological advances; and
» strong growth in the demand for convenient, fast, good-value shopping – consumers are becoming busier ("time-poor"), with more women in the workforce and an increase in the divorce rate leading to smaller families.

In Europe, outcry against the development of big stores and the threat they pose to the traditional, smaller retailers has, curiously, led to a more rapid consolidation. For example, in France restrictions on building new hypermarkets have increased, and price-control legislation was introduced in 1996. Major French chains, such as Carrefour, have sought to maintain their growth by acquisitions and also entering markets abroad, such as in Singapore, Indonesia, eastern Europe, and South America. Following a merger with Promodès, Carrefour has now become the second largest food and beverage (F&B) retailer in the world after the Dutch firm Royal Ahold. Although Wal-Mart is a much larger company, its F&B turnover is less than 20% of its total sales, so it comes third in the world F&B ranking.

Another force for consolidation was the entry of Wal-Mart into the European markets. The company swallowed two medium-sized German chains (totalling 100 supermarkets) and then, in 1999, acquired the third largest UK chain, Asda, for £6.7bn (approximately $9.5bn). Much was made of Wal-Mart's arrival at the time, but now doubts are emerging as to its capacity as a global force. Outside the US, it is a major player in only three countries – Canada, Mexico, and the UK – and its global strategy has been described by investment banker Toby Radford of JP Morgan as "rudderless." This speculation is given weight by the sudden resignation of Wal-Mart's international division head during the Asda bid.

European retailers have been extraordinarily active overseas. Royal Ahold, the Dutch group, has purchased chains in Spain, Poland, the US, and Argentina, while the UK's Tesco has opened stores in Korea. Nobody seems to be making much money out of this expansion (Carrefour, for instance, is losing money on many of its foreign operations).

Although economies of scale have fuelled mergers at home, it is not clear that they are really obtainable for retailers on a global scale. To compete effectively with existing retailers in a new market, it seems that there is a need to arrive in force – for instance, Carrefour pulled out of the US after opening only three stores, which is far below critical mass, but is established as the second largest retailer in Spain (through acquisitions). Some retail sector share-analysts are doubtful that much money can be saved in global purchasing because so many goods are made locally in the same country as the retail store – but the Euro-zone may be an exception to this rule (see below). Others argue that the savings will come from spreading marketing costs, which are increasing, as well as the cost of investment in new technology.

Eventually, the big manufacturers are likely to deal with retailers at a global level if the supermarkets are to internationalize successfully – P&G is already adopting this approach – but it is likely to be a long, slow process. Wal-Mart is the only American player with substantial international operations and even the most globalized of the European retailers earn most of their profits at home. Retailing, it seems, could be going "a bridge too far" by trying to become global.

IS THE EURO DEFLATIONARY FOR FMCG?

On the face of it, the introduction of the Euro as a common currency within the core EU nations has not had much of a deflationary effect – if anything, consumers are complaining that prices have risen as retailers across the continent have opportunistically rounded-up prices when converting to Euros. In the longer term, however, many argue that greater price transparency between the Euro-zone countries will reduce price differentials and drive the cost of retail goods downwards.

The FMCG industry is among the most vulnerable to this effect. Differences in the price of manufacturers' leading brands can be more than 30% across Europe, and retailers are blaming their suppliers for keeping wholesale prices high where they can get away with it. Larger retailers may start to switch brands in order to get better discounts, but it is not clear whether they will pass these savings on to the consumer. At present, retailers tend to buy locally from manufacturers in the same country as their stores, but in the future the larger chains may wish to make Europe-wide purchases at a single price in Euros.

FMCG manufacturer Unilever began, in 2000, to reduce the number of brands it markets down to a few hundred from its earlier portfolio of more than 1000. Other companies, such as Nestlé, are putting their group brand name on more and more of their products, apparently as part of an effort to maintain the value of the products in the customer's eyes.

But do consumers really care, and are they prepared to travel to another country to purchase goods cheaper? If the British experience is anything to go by, they certainly are. UK duty on alcohol and cigarettes is high, but for several years UK residents have been allowed to bring generous amounts of these goods home from elsewhere in the EU, provided that they are for personal use. Every day, hordes of British shoppers travel to Calais to load up with cigarettes and alcohol, as well as gourmet foods, such as French cheeses, that are more expensive and hard to find at home. Large superstores have mushroomed around Calais, specifically to serve this market. With the small size of many continental countries and good cross-border communications, it is conceivable that this phenomenon could occur elsewhere in Europe, unless prices become more uniform.

In the past, it was difficult for consumers to compare prices across the continent because they were denominated in different currencies, but now the discrepancies are all too obvious, and are likely to dwarf the price transparency effect of the Internet. Newspapers and magazines are an obvious example – in every major city, papers in a multitude of languages are easy to obtain, all with their cover price listed in different countries. A customer can hardly avoid noticing that, for instance, Britain's *Guardian* newspaper costs €2.13 in France, €2.61 in the Netherlands, and €1.67 in Portugal. And frequent travelers are likely to spot that while branded aspirin costs €3.70 in Greece, it costs €12.90 in Italy.

Although various industry spokespeople put up a brave show of justifying these differences as being due to variations in local taxes and transport costs, it is clear that both suppliers and retailers tend to charge what they can get away with, and do their best to disguise the differences. Rebates, credit terms, and other manufacturers' incentives make it very hard even for competitors in the industry to discover what their rivals are really paying.

It remains to be seen how the major players will react, but the smart money seems to be on price deflation, given that Europeans are increasingly aware of how expensive life is for them compared with most of the rest of the world.

LOOKALIKE PRODUCTS – ATTACKING BRANDS

You're in the UK and you take your young children to visit their grandmother for tea, but they misbehave. Granny offers them "Puffin" chocolate-covered biscuits from Asda, "Classic Cola" from Sainsbury's, and "Unbelievable" butter spread from Tesco, all of which they refuse to eat. Why? These products are packaged to imitate well-known brands – United Biscuits' "Penguin" biscuits, Coca-Cola, and "I Can't Believe It's Not Butter" spread – but they taste different. Granny is one of the 21% of UK consumers who have purchased products believing them to be something else (NOP survey, *Marketing* magazine, May 12, 1994). She may also be one of the many consumers who think that lookalike products are made by the same manufacturer as the brand they copy.

In the UK alone, lookalikes are worth £1.5bn ($2bn) in sales annually, some 2% of total grocery revenues. They are most prevalent in the FMCG product areas and are generally, but not always, manufactured by major retailers. The main motive is obvious – a lookalike gets a "free ride" on the massive investment in brand-building that the original manufacturer makes. Often lookalikes are of inferior quality but give the impression that they are equivalent to, or almost as good as, the known brand.

Legal protection for brands varies from country to country, and UK law is comparatively weak in this area. The act of "passing off" one product as another is narrowly interpreted and difficult to prove, while litigation can be prohibitively expensive. P&G, for example, abandoned legal action against a number of lookalikes mimicking its cleaning product Flash, and redesigned the package in 1992. The next year, new lookalikes appeared, and when P&G redesigned again in 1994, yet another generation of imitations sprang up.

Retailers with a wide range of own-label goods have a lot to gain from imitation. They may still stock the original brand in their stores to attract customers, but then use category management techniques, such as the careful positioning of the competing products, to ensure healthy sales for the lookalikes. The UK retailers are the most domestically powerful – and profitable – in Europe, and, as "gatekeepers" to the consumers, leave manufacturers with little choice but to accept the situation. The top five UK retailers control nearly 70% of chain-store grocery sales.

For the consumer who can tell the difference, the short-term effect is arguably to increase choice. We do not always wish to buy a name brand product at a premium price. In the longer term, however, if retailers continue to capture some of the revenue that would otherwise go to name brands, the quality and variety of consumer products might erode. Secondary brands could disappear, while major manufacturers might divert their product development budgets into continual repackaging of existing brands to stay one step ahead of the lookalikes.

BEST PRACTICE – PRIVATE LABELS VERSUS LEADING BRANDS

Lookalikes are only a part of the retailer's arsenal in the area of "own brands." Retail chains have been selling their own branded products, known as "own label" or "private label," since the early 1900s, but in recent years their market share has substantially increased at the expense of leading brands. Although there are no comprehensive statistics, in the US it is known that the majority of private label brands have been grabbing market share by an average of 1% a year since the mid-1990s, with sports shoes and clothing possessing approximately one-third of their respective markets by 2000. In Europe, where retailing is more concentrated, private label annual sales rose by 28% between 1993 and 1998, while the UK's private labels increased market share overall from 16.4% to 30%.

The trend is particularly strong in FMCG goods. Private labels, and manufacturers' brands that are not heavily advertised, tend to sell for less than the leading brands. The question of why consumers are willing to pay substantially more for leading brands has been extensively studied. One explanation is that consumers are "risk-averse" (don't want to make a mistake) and appreciate the consistency of quality that most leading brands seem to have. Yet this does not explain why consumers are willing to pay more for physically identical goods just because they are in a leading brand's package.

In a study in 2000 of why consumers paid more for a leading brand than its private-label competitor, shoppers were asked to rate two competing brands for quality and then asked to say how much they would pay for the private brand relative to the price of the leading brand. The shoppers turned out to have remarkably accurate perceptions of quality (correlated to objective quality measures), but even when they could see no difference in quality between two competing products, they were still willing to pay an average of 28.1% more for the leading brand. The researcher, Raj Sethuraman, thought that this was due to consumer goodwill towards the leading brands and recommended manufacturers to focus on "image-based emotional advertising" to maintain their lead, arguing that retailers would be unable to close the price gap even if they were successful in closing the quality gap.

Retailers have indeed been improving the quality of their own-label products. Today, some even offer two own-label brands at different prices – one at a low price and lower quality, and another, for example Safeway's "Select" brand, that is promoted as being as good as, or better than, leading brands. Private labels with high market share tend to enjoy better consistency in quality and also a price that is close to the premium brand's.

Most retailers say that their gross profit margins are higher on their private labels than on the leading brands they sell, even where they are able to obtain heavy discounts on purchases of leading brands. While leading brand manufacturers want to make their products so desirable that retailers cannot afford not to stock them, the retailers themselves would like a piece of the action, especially in FMCG where competition is fierce and profit margins are low. Private labels have the advantage over non-branded goods because they are more difficult to compare with products offered by competing stores.

For major retail chains, developing private labels is a way of taking control of more of the stock that they sell. Once private labels are established, they can be expanded into other categories through the "umbrella effect," potentially increasing profit margins. A good private label is also a way of differentiating a chain from competing retailers, which is becoming increasingly important.

Developing a private label is more attractive than selling less well-known manufacturers' brands because there is no "free rider" effect. If a lesser manufacturer's brand becomes successful, there is a danger that the retailer will lose any exclusive rights to the product and be squeezed on price by competitors. According to one Wal-Mart executive, "in time I believe you will see only two offerings per category on the shelf – the national brand leader and the store brand. There will be no space available for the second or third brand player in the category" (Peter Berlinski (1997) "Wal-Mart Sets New Paradigm for Private Label Success," *Private Label*, pp. 15–19). It is the weaker national and regional brands that are losing out most to the private labels, both in the US and the UK.

Private brands compete with leading brands in three main areas: price, positioning, and quality.

» **Price** – although retailers have considerable leeway in pricing their own-label goods, the larger the difference in price compared with the leading brand, the more consumers perceive the private label to be of inferior quality. Own-label price-cuts do not hurt leading brands as much as a leading brand price-cut will hurt own-label sales. One study (S.K Dhar & S.J. Hoch (1997) "Why Store Brand Penetration Varies by Retailer," *Marketing Science*, pp. 208–227) found that "a 10% change in the price gap fraction results in a 0.8% change in store brand share."

» **Positioning** – the retailer has final say on where goods are placed in the store. One study (S.J. Hoch, A.L. Montgomery & Y.-H. Park (2002) "Why the Private Label is One of the Few Brands to Show Consistent Long Term") found that promotional display during the first year of introduction was the only significantly effective way to increase market share in the second year, apparently because it increased the number of trial buyers who later became regular purchasers. The promotional display effect is even stronger for leading brands, however, and they also have two other effective promotional tools: advertising and coupons. Although some retailers advertise their own brands nationally, such as Sears and JC Penney in the US, for most it is uneconomic.

» **Quality** – in general, leading brands tend to dominate innovation, in which they have a competitive advantage. A successful innovation can dramatically increase market share in the short to medium term, until imitators can get up to speed. Retailers do not have the economies of scale to fund innovation, so they usually follow the manufacturers' lead. There are occasional exceptions, however – Co-op Superstores in the UK was the first to introduce liquid detergent capsules, in advance of P&G and Unilever.

KEY LEARNING POINTS

» The principal FMCG retailers, the supermarket chains, are at a very early stage of globalization. Most consolidation has occurred in Europe and the US.

» US retailers are not major players internationally. It is the European stores that have expanded abroad, partly in response to Wal-Mart's entry into Europe, the only American chain that is substantially active in foreign countries. It remains to be seen whether these foreign operations will be profitable in the long term.

» Within the EU itself, the advent of the Euro and the abolition of internal trade barriers have encouraged the major retailers to consolidate at home. Price transparency due to the Euro may drive prices down.

» Retailers are encroaching on leading brands, both with "looka-likes" that are generally not of the same quality, and, increasingly, with "private label" brands that are often as good as the leading brands but often cost less. If their attempts at globalization succeed, key battles will be fought between manufacturers and retailers in this area.

The State of the Art

» The trouble with trade promotions.
» Managing shelf space better.
» What kinds of promotions do retailers really want?

THE TROUBLE WITH TRADE PROMOTIONS

In spite of all the brave talk about co-operation within the industry, the reality is that relationships between manufacturers and retailers are frequently acrimonious. The majority of retailers emphasize buying cheaply, reward their managers for doing so, and maintain substantial excess capacity in storage and transportation systems to hold extra stock that they have bought on the cheap. Manufacturers have difficulty in finding ways of maintaining higher prices, since their competitors are likely to undercut them and often cannot discover how much of any special discounts they offer actually gets through to the consumer.

Greater co-operation between manufacturers and retailers should, in theory, lead to higher profits for everyone. The problem is in establishing a stable system of collaboration. With both sides rewarding managers for, in effect, outwitting the other side, rather than on maximizing profitability, there is a need for change in organizational culture.

Trade promotions are supposed to be a team effort, yet both manufacturers and retailers find them hugely frustrating. According to authors R. Blattberg and S. Neslin, in their book *Sales Promotions Concepts, Methods and Strategies*, Prentice Hall (1990), manufacturers think that only about 16% of trade promotions are profitable in the US, while the majority of retailers think that manufacturers are giving their competitors better trade-promotion deals. From the retailer's viewpoint, trade promotions are wasteful because they cost a lot in terms of administration and carrying stock. Both sides think that the schemes are highly inefficient. Despite their unprofitability, manufacturers' salespeople spend an estimated 25% of their time dealing with promotions.

In a trade promotion, the manufacturer offers the retailer a product at a lower price for a short period. The retailer is supposed to pass on this discount to the customer. The idea is that the manufacturer will generate new customers and build brand loyalty, while the retailer will sell more of the product without losing any profit margin or suffering extra expense. That's the theory – in practice, both sides tend to try to outwit the other, and in doing so play a zero-sum game where nobody benefits.

"Off-invoice" promotions, where the discounts are immediately accounted for in invoices to the retailer, present a temptation. If a retailer buys as much product as possible at the cheaper promotion price, it can then store the excess and sell it later at the normal price and make extra profits, or continue to sell the product at a discount after the promotion has officially ended, which hurts the equity of the brand. Retailers also "divert" some of the excess goods by selling them to other retailers.

Buying more of a product on promotion than you actually need is called "forward-buying." As well as hurting brand equity, it has other distorting effects. It makes it hard for manufacturers to forecast demand, since retailers are buying more than they are likely to sell, creating the opposite effect to "just-in-time" delivery. Production fluctuates wildly, and there is a lot of excess stock held in the system. But as long as the cost of holding the excess stock is less than the extra savings they make, retailers will want to keep doing it.

Trade promotions, it seems, hurt manufacturers, so why do they keep on running them? There are several reasons:

» increasing brand awareness;
» moving excess stock;
» reaching price-sensitive consumers; and
» competing against rival brands.

The solution may be in designing trade promotions that are more optimally beneficial for both sides. One attempt to do this is the introduction of "pay-for-performance," where discounts are linked to the volume of product that is actually sold during the promotion. The technology is in place – scanner data of what has sold on promotion gives an exact figure, if the retailer is willing to share the information. Most retailers aren't, however. Forward-buying works for them, so they are unlikely to co-operate in any new type of promotion that doesn't give them additional benefits. "Scan-back" promotions, as they are called, remove the incentive to forward-buy or divert because the retailer only gets a discount on what is actually sold. They also prevent the retailer from continuing the promotion after it has officially ended.

Even if the manufacturer can strong-arm the retailer into accepting scan-backs, they may still fail because the retailer "cheats." There are reports that some retailers run products several times through a scanner to boost the sales figures, while others purchase diverted goods at discount from other retailers and then sell them during a promotion for a further discount from the manufacturer. Although it may be possible to use an independent auditor to monitor the process, there is still plenty of scope for trickery.

The way out may be in offering better scan-back deals. According to marketing professors David R. Bell and Xavier Drèze, one unnamed brand leader ran a successful experiment where four selected retailers were given up to four scan-back and four off-invoice promotions of the most popular brands at different times over a year. The scan-backs gave a better discount than the off-invoices, to compensate the retailers for being unable to buy forward. The results showed that the retailers were indeed dealing in "diverted" goods – one retailer sold 20% less than it bought from the manufacturer during the year, while another, in a different region, sold 335% more of the product than it ordered! Only one of the four retailers sold roughly the same amount as it had purchased.

The scan-back deals in the trial were, however, promising, stabilizing the size of orders and allowing 75% of the discounts to actually reach the consumer, compared with 20–30% for off-invoice promotions. The manufacturer concerned is said to now be rolling out scan-back promotions elsewhere.

MANAGING SHELF SPACE BETTER

A large supermarket may carry more than 45,000 different SKUs, which makes the task of allocating shelf space extraordinarily difficult. For the retailer, getting the manufacturers to pay premiums for the best spaces makes it easier to make profitable decisions, but not necessarily the optimal ones. Eager for more and better spaces, manufacturers are willing to spend large sums on obtaining temporary promotional space in "gondolas" (in the aisles), end-caps, and front walls. In some categories, such as cigarettes, manufacturers commonly make long-term "rent" agreements for space, with the leading manufacturer paying more and obtaining the most space.

The reason why positioning is so important is the overwhelming evidence that consumers don't walk into a store knowing exactly what they are going to buy (only about one-third of purchases are pre-planned). Once in the store, they generally make decisions quickly, without comparing prices very carefully, and have generally "low involvement" in the process. Furthermore, shoppers tend to go to supermarkets more than once a week, and their spending on any particular visit is "elastic," meaning that they may spend a lot or a little. What this all amounts to is that it is possible to influence the consumer's purchases dramatically by attracting their attention while they are in the store.

The challenge for the retailer is how to maximize the amount shoppers spend in their store on each visit by manipulating their attention. This can be done by music (one study found that slowing the tempo of in-store music reduced the pace at which customers shop), smells, such as baking bread, and visual displays and positioning.

Stores tend to be visually confusing, with a large number of displays competing with one another for the customer's attention. Surprisingly little is known about how effective different approaches to managing space really are, and many retailers opt for methods that are primarily intended to reduce the amount of time staff spend moving items around on the shelves.

An ambitious study by researchers from the University of Chicago in 60 stores of a Chicago supermarket chain in 1994 sought to test various ways in which better micro-management of shelf organization might increase sales. The chain was spread across inner city and suburban areas, and customers formed four socio-economic clusters – inner-city urban, blue-collar urban, established suburbs, and younger suburbs – but eventually it was found that the relevant distinction was between urban and suburban stores. Using software programs to design optimal "planograms," the layout of floor space and shelf space in each store, the researchers changed the size of facings, the height of shelves, removed some slow-moving items and repositioned some products. For example, the researchers increased the amount of automatic dishwasher detergent in the suburban stores compared with the urban stores. Certain stores in each cluster were left unchanged as a control.

Next, the researchers rearranged two pairs of complementary goods in two different categories, oral care and laundry. While toothpaste and detergent were repurchased on average every two months, toothbrushes were bought on average only every four to six months, and fabric softener was bought by far fewer customers. The aim was to see if it was possible to sell more of the slower-moving items (toothbrushes and fabric softener) by positioning them nearer to fast-moving complementary items (toothpaste and detergent, respectively). Toothbrushes, which had been on the top shelves, were moved to eye level while some toothpaste items went to the top shelves. Originally, laundry products had been arranged side by side, from liquid detergent to powder detergent to fabric softener. The researchers placed the fabric softener in between the two types of detergent.

Another series of tests sought to "manipulate the ease of shopping" by, for instance, making it harder for shoppers to compare the prices of differently sized packages of same-brand toilet rolls by moving them further away from one another, while cereals and condensed soup were reorganized to make it easier for shoppers to find their preferred flavors.

The study found that the changes produced an average increase of 3.9% in dollar terms across the eight categories tested. The researchers point out that this was an increase in items being sold at full price, not on promotion, and that it amounts to a substantial increase in annual sales. For a category selling $2000 a week per store at a 25% profit, for instance, a 3% increase would result in an extra annual profit of $67,000, far more than the additional expense of designing the planograms.

For the complementary merchandising tests, the study found that moving toothbrushes to eye level increased sales by 8% without hurting toothpaste sales (some toothpaste was moved to the top shelves). Overall, all the laundry products increased sales, by 5% overall.

In the ease of shopping tests, the test strategies produced mixed results. While making it harder for shoppers to compare toilet tissue prices increased sales by 5%, arranging Campbell's Soup varieties alphabetically resulted in a drop of 6%; while rearranging cereals, which had been organized by manufacturer, into adult, kids, and all-the-family sections produced a drop of 5%. Puzzled, the researchers interviewed shoppers to investigate why, and found that they had virtually no awareness of how the sections were organized (neither in the test layouts nor in the control layouts), they found them confusing, and were unaware that the layouts had been changed in the test layouts.

The researchers speculate that the reason for the drop in sales was that they had inadvertently reduced impulse purchasing by making it too easy for customers to find what they wanted.

All this is of interest to both retailers and manufacturers, but manufacturers have a further interest, which is in seeing how changes in shelf position affect sales of individual brands. The study found that while eye level position was generally thought to be the best position, business people defined eye level differently, ranging from "above the knees" to below six-and-a-half feet. There was also disagreement among manufacturers over whether the middle or the ends of shelves were better. The study found that, in general, products had too much space allocated – the number of facings a product had was the least important factor, and above a certain limit, which varied from category to category, more space had no effect on sales at all.

What really mattered was the vertical position – 51–53 inches off floor was the best, which, the researchers point out, tallies with Kodak's rule that the preferred viewing angle lies 15 degrees below the horizontal. In other words, the best place to put products is slightly below eye level. An exception to this was in the refrigerated section, where the "well," the bottom of the case which projects out into the aisle, was the best.

Another finding was that a brand could improve its sales by 15% by moving from the worst to the best position horizontally and 39% by moving vertically. However, retailers don't have the staff to micro-manage more than a few categories, and there is a constant flow of new and different products, so the potential for improvement is likely to be much smaller – the researchers suggest an overall 4–5% improvement in category sales is realistic for the US, but point out that high overheads in the UK make shelf space more costly, so the potential for gains may be greater.

WHAT KINDS OF PROMOTIONS DO RETAILERS REALLY WANT?

It's often hard to know which promotions are really effective because they are so frequently "footballs" in the ongoing price negotiations between suppliers and retailers. A retailer may go along with a promotion, for instance, not because he thinks it will work but because he hopes to buy a large amount of products at a deep discount and sell it off at a quick profit to other stores. Staff in retail outlets often express very different opinions about what works, and may not have access to enough information to form an accurate judgment.

A 1999 survey by Cornell University sought to explore the real views of retailing executives about which promotions really worked, and which were non-starters. While some of their results were predictable – for example, that giving out free samples in-store increased sales – others were surprising. The researchers point out that while manufacturers use promotions in the hope of increasing or maintaining sales volume and market share, retailers want to increase store traffic and customer loyalty and to improve profits within categories, and they argue that manufacturers need a better understanding of what the retailers prefer.

The survey found that the most widely used promotions were, in descending order:

» in-store demos and sampling;
» shipper displays;
» promotions for local charities;
» co-operative radio advertising;
» in-store coupons;
» retailer shelf-talkers;
» targeted direct mail;
» in-store advertising;
» in-ad coupons; and
» tear pads.

Local charity promotions, although the third most commonly used promotion, were generally perceived as being ineffective – retailers do it to maintain a good image with their customers, rather than in the hope of selling more products. Tear pads were also seen as doing almost nothing to increase sales, but are provided as a service to the customer.

So which promotions did the retailers really like?

» Targeted direct mail – sent to specific customers, retailers thought this was the best promotion overall.

» Shipper displays – these are display units that are supplied by the manufacturer with product already inside. They were regarded as very effective, particularly by larger chains.

» Co-operative radio and TV advertising – with the large number of local stations in the US, this kind of advertising can be inexpensive, and retailers felt that these ads helped to increase overall sales.

» Frequent-shopper schemes – 62% of the retailers use these schemes and most said they would support them in the future.

» In-ad and in-store coupons – these were seen to be highly effective.

» In-store demos and sampling – seen as a good performer, particularly by supermarkets, but there were concerns that they do not generate customer loyalty to the store.

Apart from mass merchandisers, who preferred TV and radio ads paid partly by the manufacturer (''co-operative''), most retailers agreed that coupons, shipper displays and display space bought by manufacturers were the schemes that they would be most likely to support.

KEY LEARNING POINTS

» Most trade promotions are off-invoice, which means that retailers get the extra discount on any amount of the product they purchase during the promotion period. This produces a loophole which many of them exploit, first by ''diverting,'' which means buying more product than they need and selling the excess to other retailers at slightly higher than the promotional discount price, and second, by buying excess promotional product and selling it later at the full price, or continuing to run the promotion after it is supposed to have finished. One leading brand manufacturer found that a store sold 335% more product during a year than it actually ordered, presumably because it was purchasing from another retailer who was ''diverting.''

» Trade promotions as they are presently practiced are wildly inefficient for the industry as a whole. The solution may lie in devising pay-for-performance promotions that are attractive enough for retailers to abandon the present off-invoice schemes.

» Customers only know what they are going to buy before they enter a store a third of the time. Once they are inside, they make their choices quickly and with "low involvement." Since they go to supermarkets frequently, they have a lot of discretion as to which trip to spend the most money on. All this points to the potential for stores to influence what customers buy through sensory cues. In supermarkets, however, so many rival products are screaming for attention that many messages may get lost.

» Eye-level shelf space – slightly below the average horizontal view at 51–53 inches off the floor – is almost certainly the best position for most products. Horizontal position is much less important.

» Matching complementary products – especially one fast-mover and one slow-mover, e.g., toothpaste and toothbrushes – seems to be effective, especially if the slower-mover gets the better shelf position.

» Making displays too user-friendly, however, may be self-defeating, possibly because it reduces the amount of impulse purchasing. On the other hand, making things slightly more difficult, for example by positioning products to make price comparisons take longer, seems to work well in terms of increased sales.

» In one survey of what types of promotion retailers prefer, coupons, frequent-shopper schemes, targeted mailshots, and shipper displays (products supplied by the manufacturer in their own display units) scored very highly. Of these, coupons are perhaps the most attractive from the manufacturer's point of view.

In Practice –
FMCG-Selling Success
Stories

» The Red Bull generation.
» FMCG in east Asia.
» Carbonated soft drinks (CSD) in the US – Coke and Pepsi.

THE RED BULL GENERATION

Mass-marketing theory developed in an era when the archetypal FMCG consumer was a white middle-class American housewife with a stable and predictable set of values. The extraordinary diversity of consumers today is a function of success. Quite simply, as the world has become more prosperous, a much wider range of people across the globe has gained access to consumer goods. Not only have social norms changed in the US, but newer consumer markets challenge marketers to find novel ways of appealing to them. The emergence of the global youth market – affluent, demanding, and mercurial – defies FMCG firms to keep up with them.

Every marketing person knows this, but some of the most successful recent product innovations have come out of nowhere, rather than from the heavily-funded R&D departments of the major brand manufacturers and multimillion dollar mass-advertising campaigns.

In 1987, Red Bull, a tiny Austrian firm, launched a drink at the youth market that now achieves over $1bn in sales worldwide – with virtually no mass-market advertising – and established a new product category in the process. The "energy drink" has pulled this off without substantially engaging with the US market, which it is only now beginning to penetrate.

A case of beginner's luck? Not really – Red Bull's founder, Dietrich Mateschitz, was for many years the international marketing manager for the German toothpaste manufacturer Blendax, recently purchased by P&G. In the early 1980s, Mateschitz was struck by an article about a Japanese tonic-drink manufacturer, Taisho Pharmaceuticals, which is so successful that it is the country's largest taxpayer. He had a candidate of his own in mind – a very cheap Thai energy booster, much loved by heavy manual workers, called Krating Daeng (Thai for "red bull"). The syrup rights were owned by Blendax's Thai licensee, Chaleo Yoovidhya.

Mateschitz and Yoovidhya set up Red Bull as equal owners and went to work adapting the Krating Daeng recipe to Western taste. After three years, the proportions seemed right – a combination of taurine, an amino acid lost during high physical and mental stress that acts as a metabolic transmitter; glucuronolactone, a detoxifier; caffeine; sucrose; glucose; and B vitamins.

Mateschitz is an energetic sportsman, keen on flying, moto-cross, and snowboarding. He used to drink Krating Daeng to recover from jetlag in Thailand, and was certain that the Red Bull version would appeal to Europe's rave-going generation who needed the stamina to keep going at all-night parties. Conventional marketing approaches were unlikely to create the right image. Europe's educated youth market is said to be deeply anti-corporate-America and resistant to widely advertised items – a product is more "cool" if only a few people know about it and the manufacturer is "credible" (i.e., not a multinational). Mateschitz approached student union representatives and offered them free cases of Red Bull on the condition that they threw parties and gave the drink away. It wasn't an original strategy, but the Ecstasy-taking generation loved the product, and it worked.

Packaging was an important factor. Red Bull comes in "slimcans," 250ml cans that are smaller than normal, but customers think the size makes it look concentrated. Marc Gobe, president and CEO of the Desgrippes Gobe group, a New York branding firm, calls the slimcan an "anti-Pepsi statement" and says that "Red Bull doesn't have any of the commercial trappings of a traditional, off-the-shelf product. It's underground, even when it's above ground."

Unlike Krating Daeng, Red Bull isn't cheap, at $2 per slimcan (it's a high-margin product), but European rave-goers have flocked to "full moon parties" in Thailand, sponsored by Red Bull in hippie enclaves such as the island of Koh Samui. Red Bull continues to position itself successfully as an anti-establishment, "in the know," anti-brand brand, while growing at an astonishing pace. Achieving 0.2 billion unit sales in 1997, it reached 1.6 billion units in 2001 across 62 countries and shows no sign of slowing. Krating Daeng, meanwhile, basks in its reflected glory and has substantially increased its own market share in Thailand.

Red Bull's other image angle is to promote itself as "extreme." It sponsors high-risk sports such as flying, car racing, and cliff-diving, which it somewhat disingenuously claims are for the athletes' benefit alone. For a "non-marketed" brand, the firm spends a considerable amount on marketing – some 35% of turnover in 2001.

As sales have increased, so have the problems. Critics have blamed a number of deaths at parties on the product, and France has banned it altogether. In Japan, Red Bull could only be sold at pharmacies for some years, while Norway classifies it as a medicine. However, the all-important Food and Drug Administration in the US, which is not known for any reluctance to ban potentially dangerous products, has not forbidden the drink, and the current consensus is that Red Bull will ride out the health scares.

The competition

Other soft-drink makers are trying to cash in on energy drinks. Coca-Cola, PepsiCo, and Anheuser-Busch (makers of Budweiser) have all launched rival products, while a host of smaller firms have introduced brands such as Dark Dog, Energy Bomb, Blue Ox, Hard E, Whoop Ass, Virgin Hi Energy, and SoBe Lean, which have been greeted with derision by hardcore Red Bull fans.

So far, the competitors have not made much headway – Red Bull still has an estimated 85% of the global market and has become the trendy thing to mix with vodka at nightclubs from New York to Jakarta. Bars were initially resistant to stocking Red Bull because of its high price – in the US, the wholesale price is around $1.33 – and the difficulty of stock control because of the small size of the cans. According to Oliver Paine, manager of a trendy San Fransisco bar, employees drink many cans while they work – six cans of Red Bull is "$10 in money that really equates to $70 of lost sales ... [it] is the same as them drinking an entire bottle of vodka for us."

A Red Bull distributor in Australia, Sydneywide Distributors Pty Ltd, was successfully sued by Red Bull in 2001 when it introduced a rival brand named LiveWire. Sydneywide had claimed that it was unaware of the similarities between the packaging of LiveWire and Red Bull (in particular, the color, diagonal lines, and layout) but LiveWire design sketches were produced containing notes by a director indicating his awareness of the resemblance.

One interesting feature of the case was the evidence given by an expert witness, psychologist Dr George Beaton, who said that consumers behave differently when purchasing FMCG goods than they do when they buy other products. According to Beaton, FMCG buyers tend to walk down supermarket aisles looking quickly for their brands, using the product's overall brand identity or "Gestalt" in order to spot the desired item. Beaton's view was that LiveWire's Gestalt was similar enough to Red Bull's for consumers to be deceived – some consumers are likely to see lookalike products as being the same brand, or coming from the same manufacturer.

KEY LEARNING POINTS

» Knowing your market means just that – knowing the customers well enough to respect them and understand their values. Like most consumers, young people are sick of the patronising tone of so many ad campaigns and have a sixth sense about authenticity. Red Bull appeals as being dangerous, rebellious, and exciting and has managed to associate itself with the "underground" without saying so overtly. Many marketing clichés derive from 1950s America, when consumers genuinely saw the availability of consumer goods as a sign of increasing prosperity, a view that is now only held in developing countries that are only now gaining access to these products. Red Bull's selling approach recognizes the modern consumer's jaded view of brands.

» Red Bull's brand equity is powerful enough to overcome price resistance. It is expensive and comes in small quantities, yet these characteristics are associated by its consumers with high quality, not high margins.

» One of the reasons why industry observers believe that Red Bull will survive the health scares is that its customers are not afraid to take a risk – one loyal consumer of the drink remarks, "I know I am abusing my body, but I am still young."

» In his evidence during Red Bull's court case against its Australian lookalike, expert witness Dr George Beaton described consumers as having "low involvement" in their purchases of FMCG. In other words, customers tend to know the brands they want and don't wish to spend any more time than necessary in purchasing them. Even if your customers love your product, don't expect them to care as much about it as you do.

» Mateschitz himself drinks an unsweetened version of the drink, yet he says that he will never market it – Western consumers continue to expect heavily sweetened food and drink, and Mateschitz isn't going to try to change their minds. Red Bull has been described as a "non-marketed" brand, yet this is untrue – it has been superbly targeted at an appropriate niche market for whom mass-advertising is inappropriate.

FMCG IN EAST ASIA

Consumer-driven economies are relatively new in Asia and present special challenges for FMCG. It's not that the demand isn't there – the major cities are studded with ultra-modern mega-malls selling a vast range of desirable products, while brand leaders use middlemen to penetrate even the most troubled areas, moving goods through black markets along the Mekong River, through Indo-China's infamous Golden Triangle, trading successfully in Indonesia despite near civil war and opening up joint-venture factories in the pariah state of North Korea. In the handful of primitive villages of the virtually uninhabited Mergui archipelago, off the coast of Myanmar, it is still possible to purchase familiar brands of soft drink, cigarettes, and chewing gum. With China opening up, there is a staggering potential demand for well-known brands.

According to the research group ACNielsen, the two biggest brands in the Asia-Pacific region are Coca-Cola and Marlboro, selling well over a billion dollars of product a year. The other top brands are Benson & Hedges, Fanta, Kelloggs, Nescafé, and Pepsi. Growth is faster than elsewhere in the world, with a 10% increase in sales being not uncommon. For the major manufacturers, Asia-Pacific is very much a market of the future.

Until the mid-1990s, most Asian retailing was highly fragmented, a myriad of small, locally run businesses, with wholesaling and the major stores controlled by a handful of tycoons whose operations span an incredible variety of different types of business. Then came the currency crisis of 1997, when devaluation spread across the region in a domino effect that wiped out countless businesses and threw the banking systems into chaos. Western retail giants moved in to buy up distressed chains, such as Tesco's purchase of stores from the Thai group Charoen Pokphand.

The Western retailers have an advantage in their superior technology and experience in running megastores, and at the time it seemed that they would easily achieve dominance across the region, with property going for a song and local stock markets in chaos. Some retailers, such as Carrefour and Royal Ahold, had already been active before the crisis and were soon joined by others, such as Wal-Mart Casino and Tesco.

Royal Ahold established itself solidly in Thailand, then bought chains in Malaysia and Singapore and set up joint ventures in Indonesia and Shanghai, increasing its stores in the region from 40 in 1998 to 150 in 1999. Then suddenly the company announced that it was pulling out of China, Indonesia, and Singapore because there was no prospect of making a profit in the medium term. In Shanghai, for example, the local supermarkets had been very much the second choice for shoppers, who preferred to buy food at the traditional "wet markets." Royal Ahold had moved in to set up 45 Tops supermarkets, aiming to attract customers by offering even fresher produce than was available in the wet markets. The project worked. Then two local chains, Lian Hua and Hua Lian, rapidly expanded the number of stores they controlled, to 450, dwarfing Royal Ahold's 45 stores, by obtaining preferential treatment from local government officials, and adopted Royal Ahold's strategy of offering very fresh produce. This was all great news for the local consumer, but Royal Ahold, like so many foreign companies in China, had been outmaneuvered. Global strategies may sound great in boardrooms and shareholders' meetings back home, but in developing countries people don't necessarily play by the same rules. Even overseas Chinese commonly complain that it is extremely hard for an outsider to make money in mainland China.

Carrefour and Wal-Mart are still expanding in China at the time of writing. Much of their produce is purchased locally, and local suppliers like doing business with these large, well-run firms that offer a huge potential distribution. It's still easy to make mistakes, though, as when Wal-Mart attempted to sell clothes in American sizes, which are too large for the locals. Some industry pundits think that Wal-Mart has particular difficulty in adapting to the needs of local consumers throughout the whole region.

Hong Kong and the Philippines have been problematic for other reasons. Hong Kong retailing is controlled by the tycoon Li Ka Shing and the venerable firm of Jardine Matheson, a trading house with its origins in the nineteenth century. Carrefour, which has been successful elsewhere, withdrew from Hong Kong after being unable to break the duopoly. Until recently foreign retailers were forbidden in the Philippines and Carrefour and others have decided not to enter the market, largely, it seems, because of the political risks.

Carrefour is probably the most experienced of the Western interlopers – it has been in Asia the longest – and is the most widespread. Each of its hypermarkets is run as a profit center, and it tends to have only a few stores in each country. For consumers, Carrefour is attractive because it offers a "wet market style" in its fresh produce departments, with the bonus of air-conditioning and hygienic conditions.

Air-conditioned megastores are particularly attractive to consumers in hotter parts of the region. People like their traditional markets, but they also like to get out of the sun. In Kuala Lumpur, for example, all life seems to revolve around the malls, where people go to stroll, eat, meet friends, and occasionally buy things, away from the blistering heat outside.

Asian consumers love value and novelty. Watsons, a drugstore chain based in Hong Kong that is spreading across the region, has something to teach the Western firms – although it is supposed to be a pharmacy, its stores are a chaotic riot of conflicting categories, from greetings cards to cosmetics, and it is the top toy retailer in Asia. Boots the Chemist, with the pseudo-clinical feel to its stores, may have to change – in Japan, for example, it discovered that customers find it offensive to give money to cashiers who are sitting down. Japanese retailer Ito-Yokado 7-Eleven is a pioneer of the convenience store, which has taken the rest of Asia by storm – in many places, consumers only have the wet markets and convenience stores to choose from.

It is far too early to see who the real winners in retailing will be. Many people applaud Carrefour, but investment bank Morgan Stanley criticized the group in a survey for choosing bad locations and selling lines in ways that are "too French." With novelty being such an important factor, the results so far may be deceptive – Asian shoppers will flock to new stores, but are not necessarily loyal.

Before the currency crisis, local businesses found it far too easy to borrow money from banks that were plagued by political interference and cronyism. Today, as the region recovers, there is a consumer credit boom that looks just as shaky. With virtually no credit information, banks know next to nothing about their customers. Hong Kong currently has the world's highest credit card default rate, with the average defaulter owing 55 months' worth of income, compared with 21 months in America. With virtually no legal system for small claims and repossessions, it is hard to see how banks across the region will deal with bad consumer loans. Another economic hiccup could hurt retailers very seriously indeed if shoppers are forced to return to the local wet markets.

A major problem may be in the competition between the Western firms themselves. Although Asia is wide open, with a tiny number of hypermarkets by Western standards, the giants are opening a huge number of stores in the most obvious locations and are already waging price wars. As with other industries, such as electronics, Asia is likely to leapfrog stages of development and learn all it can from Western methods. Like interlopers from earlier times, such as Jardine Matheson, some Western firms may well succeed in becoming standard fixtures of the retail scene as they integrate themselves with local ways. Others may fail as the notion that a standardized global approach reveals itself to be, as far as retailing is concerned, something of a paper tiger.

KEY LEARNING POINTS

» Leading brand manufacturers are among the most sophisticated global players around, and have decades of experience in reaching bizarre and remote markets. In Asia, brands such as Coca-Cola and Marlboro are well-adapted to local distribution channels and are growing strongly. The future looks bright for them in Asia, where retail power so far represents no challenge.

» Western retailers, mainly from Europe, entered the region in force during the 1990s. They have advantages in terms of their buying power, logistical excellence, and megastore expertise, but are up against some very savvy local rivals who have better links with government – and in much of Asia, governmental cronyism is still the main way to get things done.

> » While local consumers welcome novelty, they expect some adaptation to local tastes, and Western retailers have understandably made mistakes. So far, their big success is in being able to offer fresh produce more hygienically than what is available in the local wet markets. As long as they can get good fresh produce, many shoppers seem to prefer the clean, bright, air-conditioned environments that the supermarkets offer.
> » Asian shoppers tend to be more highly price-sensitive than in the West, and with the retail giants beginning to compete with one another on price, it seems likely that some chains will lose out in the long term.

CARBONATED SOFT DRINKS (CSD) IN THE US – COKE AND PEPSI

The CSD industry developed in the nineteenth century (see Chapter 3) and its leading players (Coca-Cola and PepsiCo) are among the largest companies in the world. Few FMCG businesses can be said to have been more consistently successful. In the US, annual CSD sales are almost $60bn, and account for about one-third of all the liquid that Americans drink (another third consists of beer, coffee, and milk). You can buy CSDs almost everywhere, from convenience stores and garages to restaurants and vending machines. The top three "parent" firms (Coca-Cola, PepsiCo, and Cadbury Schweppes) spend over $600mn annually on advertising in the US alone, have a combined market share of 90%, are among the most widely recognized trademarks around the world, and now have a major share (over 40%) in the bottling plants that produce CSDs. From the point of view of long-term investors, these firms have outperformed the stock market by a wide margin for many decades.

Although everybody has heard of the major CSD brands, not many outside the industry understand its structure or how it has changed during the last few decades. Traditionally, the drinks were made by bottlers who bought the proprietary concentrate, known as "syrup," from the parent companies, mixed it with carbonated water to produce the finished product, and marketed it to retailers in their territories as well as selling through their own vending operations (including vending machines and "fountains" in bars and restaurants). The bottlers used their own staff to put the drinks on their retailers' shelves, price them, and supervize point-of-sale materials. The syrup itself was made by the parent firm who had exclusive contracts with the independent bottlers, and were the major advertisers of the product.

Bottling mergers

In 1960, Coca-Cola was unquestionably the dominant player in the industry. Since then, however, it has lost market share to its competitors, in particular to PepsiCo. There were major changes in the 1980s, when PepsiCo and Coca-Cola changed their system of using independent bottlers and began to buy them up while their smaller competitors got out of bottling altogether. This was the first major change to the system of independent bottlers with exclusive territories that had been in place since the late nineteenth century. During the 1980s many bottlers were acquired, either by other bottlers or by their parent firm, and the total number of US bottlers fell by more than 50% by 2000.

Why did the bottling system change? The answer seems to lie in gradually improving economies of scale. According to the Boston Consulting Group, manufacturing costs dropped by around 35% between 1950 and 1985. An improved transport infrastructure, increases in sales, an expansion of supermarkets, the development of mass-media advertising since the 1950s, the introduction of non-returnable plastic and aluminium can packages, and more efficient production lines all contributed to a fall in the per-unit cost of manufacture.

Bottlers were restricted by their franchise contracts from selling rival brands of the same "flavor," which meant that while, for example, a Coca-Cola bottler could obtain a Dr Pepper franchise because Dr Pepper is a "non-cola," it could not acquire another bottler with a franchise for Pepsi or RC Cola. In 1950 there were more than 6500 independent bottling plants in the US. Larger bottlers began to realize that they could expand sales through mergers and acquisitions while continuing to reduce their manufacturing costs per unit. Initially, the obvious acquisitions were of two kinds – either a same-brand bottler in the territory next door, or a different-brand bottler in the same territory.

Bottlers have "calendar marketing agreements" (CMAs) with supermarkets and grocers, where they pay the retailer for "feature" promotions of their product. The feature, which can last up to a month, uses advertising and special in-store displays to promote the drink at a cut price, all paid for by the bottler. Pepsi and Coke bottlers generally have exclusivity clauses in their CMAs that prohibit retailers from running promotions of competing products during the same period. There have been complaints that sometimes Pepsi and Coke have alternated their features in certain stores for as long as a year, thus keeping other rivals from running any promotions at all during the period. Features are said to account for the majority of sales in food stores, and are therefore crucially valuable to the bottlers.

As supermarket chains grew, they began to find that they were dealing with more than one bottler of the same brand, which spurred bottlers to consolidate. By 1990 the number of bottlers had shrunk to approximately 800, through mergers and acquisitions, and by 2000 there were about 500. The PepsiCo and Coca-Cola parent firms also purchased stakes in their bottlers, and are believed to own or have shares in bottlers that generate about 75% of their annual US sales. Coca-Cola set up a separate firm, Coca-Cola Enterprises, to purchase bottlers, and denies that it controls it, although many outsiders regard it as an arm of the parent firm.

Other competitors sold off their bottling interests during the same period, but in 1998 the food group Cadbury Schweppes, now the owner of Dr Pepper and 7UP, began to acquire interests in its bottlers through a joint venture with the Carlyle Group. In 1986, Coca-Cola had attempted to purchase Dr Pepper while PepsiCo tried to buy 7UP but fell foul of US anti-trust law (see below). Dr Pepper and 7UP then merged in the same year and were eventually purchased by Cadbury Schweppes in 1995.

While Coke and Pepsi remain stable players, other competitors have changed ownership frequently since the 1980s. Philip Morris, for example, purchased 7UP during the 1980s but failed in its attempt to establish "Like-Cola" as a successful brand, largely because of Coke and Pepsi's exclusivity deals with their bottlers on cola production. Royal Crown attempted to merge with the 7UP/Dr Pepper group in the 1990s but was defeated by the group's acquisition by Cadbury Schweppes.

Cadbury Schweppes is said not to wish to go to war with Coke and Pepsi in the cola business. It owns a large number of smaller soft drink brands that are non-colas (such as Canada Dry and Sunkist) that are made and distributed by Coke and Pepsi bottlers and there currently seems to be an uneasy peace between the parent firms.

Anti-trust issues

For very successful businesses, anti-monopoly laws, known in the US as "anti-trust" laws, often become a major issue. The US competition authority has taken an interesting view of the CSD problem. On one hand, it has forbidden Coke and Pepsi from buying other large CSD parents, but allowed them to purchase small CSD-makers; and on the other hand it has allowed them to integrate vertically by buying equity in their bottlers and has also allowed – or failed to prevent – horizontal integration among their bottlers.

Historically, US bottlers were given franchises in perpetuity, which meant that the concentrate companies could not force franchise transfers, except for gross misconduct – for example, poor sanitation – and forced transfers have been very rare. For the regulators, the focus of concern has been on Coke and Pepsi bottlers' acquisition of independent bottlers in the same territory. The US government has challenged many of these acquisitions on the grounds that they lead to unfairly high prices, but has not fought Coke and Pepsi's vertical integration with their own bottlers, because these moves tend to lead to lower prices for the consumer.

Abroad, Coke fell foul of competition law when a French court blocked its purchase of Orangina in 1999, while other countries around the world are concerned to prevent the firm gaining too much power in the soft drinks trade with restaurants, cafés, and hotels.

With the extraordinary size and power of the parent firms, maintaining growth is a perennial problem. The successful consolidation of their home market was a remarkable achievement, but now Coke, in particular, is faced with no more worlds to conquer, for the time being at least. Asia, with its volatile but rapidly developing economies and vast population, looks like being the next great challenge in the medium to long term.

KEY INSIGHTS

» Coke and Pepsi's remarkable ability to dominate an industry for so many decades is one of the great business success stories of all time.

» At home in the US, still the key market, the parent concentrate firms were able to avoid the attentions of the anti-trust regulators because of the curious position of the bottlers who, since the nineteenth century, had enjoyed ownership of their territorial franchises in perpetuity. Coke and Pepsi could hardly be said to be unfairly dominating a market when such a major part of the business was in the hands of third parties.

» The situation changed when bottlers started to consolidate during the 1980s, but the parent firms were allowed to gain control of many ''anchor'' bottlers, because the regulators perceived this as being good for consumers, in the sense that it tended to lower prices.

» Their defense of the ''cola'' flavor, largely through exclusivity contracts with bottlers, has proved to be a key factor in preventing others from entering the cola business. Not many firms in any industry have been able to defeat their rivals for such a long period, and there is no sign of this changing.

Key Concepts and Thinkers

» Glossary.
» Consumer boycotts.
» Malicious rumors that won't die – the P&G logo.
» Managing boycotts.

GLOSSARY

Back card – A point-of-sale card fixed to the back of a dump-bin or floor-stand, designed to give an advertising message at eye level.

Bait and switch – An American term that means advertising an item at a very low price to attract customers. Usually the item is not available, and the customer is offered a more expensive item. Illegal in many countries, including the US, but often attempted.

Best food day – The day of the week on which most food is sold. Retailers tend to place their newspaper ads on this day.

Case deal – Volume discount offered by a manufacturer based on the number of cases of a product that are purchased by the retailer.

Category killers – Usually means a large store focused on one category of product (a superstore), but is sometimes used to mean, perhaps incorrectly, the most powerful brands in a category.

Channel marketing – A way of organizing marketing functions of a company to put individuals in charge of selling certain classes of trade.

Circular coffin – In the US, a horizontal display in the frozen food section.

Closing – Action taken to gain a commitment to buy or proceed onwards towards the point where this can logically occur.

Cold calling – Approaches to potential customers by any method (face-to-face or telephone, say) who are ''cold,'' i.e., have expressed no prior interest of any sort.

Commodity – In US retailing, a product sold at less than the cost of purchase. These items are usually sold and promoted with product which has a high margin. For example, coffee is often a ''commodity'' item that is sold at a loss, but is promoted with a creamer which has a high margin.

Competitor intelligence – The information collected about competitive products and services and their suppliers that may specifically be used to improve the approach taken on a call.

Country of origin – In most countries, a label must indicate where the product was made, and this may influence customers' perception of its quality.

Cross-selling – The technique of selling across, ensuring that a range of different services are bought from a client who starts by buying only one.

Delicatessen buying – Buying a wide range of goods in small quantities, the implication being that the retailer does not appreciate, or does not wish to satisfy, consumer demand.

Display allowance – An incentive offered by the supplier to the retailer in return for off-shelf display of the product.

Display merchandiser – A permanent display unit supplied by the manufacturer, usually including a "service attachment," such as a battery tester.

Distressed product – A product that won't sell. Often sold at a loss to free shelf space. If it is perishable, the supplier usually reimburses the retailer.

Double-invoicing – Fraudulently sending two invoices.

Efficient Consumer Response – A way of studying the effectiveness of promotions, product flow, and product development to determine the profitability of a brand.

Features – The factual things to be described about a service (see also "Benefits" above) *or*, in FMCG retailing, an ad within a retailer's circular or a newspaper ad.

Football – A leading brand that is price-sensitive, where the price fluctuates frequently, such as Coca-Cola.

Forward-buying – Buying excess product at a discount to sell later at full price.

Front-end – The part of the store near the cash registers where impulse products, high-profit items, and items that are easily stolen are usually placed.

Gift with purchase (GWP) – In department stores, a free gift with what you buy, such as free eye shadow with a bottle of perfume.

Gondola – A long narrow display case from which merchandise is accessible to customers on either side.

Gondola end – A product display case designed for the end of a gondola. Usually considered a prime display.

Loss-leader – A product featured at a low price, often below cost, in order to increase store traffic to sell additional profitable items.

Low-volume product – A convenience item that is only stocked because customers appreciate it, such as shoelaces.

Performance requirements – Rules set by the manufacturer in order for a retailer to reclaim advertising costs.

Point-of-sale materials – Usually printed materials designed to attract consumer attention and stimulate a purchase at the retail store.

Private label – A retailer's own brand.

Proof of purchase – In a promotion, the requirement that the applicant prove that they bought the product, such as sending in a box-top when entering a competition.

Purchase cycle – How often people purchase an item.

Sales aids – Anything used during the sales conversation to enhance what is said, such as items, information (say, a graph), or even other people.

Sales audit – An occasional, systematic review of all aspects of sales activity and its management to identify areas needing improvement, or working well and needing extension. A process that recognizes the inherent dynamic nature of sales.

Sales productivity – The sales equivalent of productivity in an area, the focus here is on efficiencies that maximize the amount of time spent with customers, rather than traveling, writing reports, etc. It focuses on ratios and touches on anything that increases sales success, however measured.

Scanner data – Information captured by barcode scanners at checkouts, used to analyze sales and control stock.

Shelf-extender – A fixture that can hold additional product on the shelf to create extra product visibility and availability.

Shelf-talker – Information displayed with the product. It may give suggestions on how to use the product or promote competitions.

Shrinkage – Loss of merchandise due to theft.

Split-out – How a retail chain distributes products around its stores. A central buyer may purchase, say, 5000 cases of sweets and then split out 50 cases to each store.

Territory – The area covered by an individual salesperson. It is usually, but not always, geographic.

CONSUMER BOYCOTTS

With all the focus on appealing to consumers as they shop, it's easy to forget that there are wider ideological and political issues that may affect what they buy. In this chapter, we will look at the extraordinary increase in the number of well-organized boycotts of FMCG products.

Although not new (see Chapter 3), consumer boycotts have become increasingly important during the last few years. Since all parties involved have an incentive to distort the facts, their effectiveness is difficult to measure, but it is clear that many campaigns have a powerful influence on consumer behavior and can seriously damage the sales and image of targeted firms. FMCG are particularly vulnerable, since by definition they are the goods that consumers most often encounter.

Boycotts are becoming more focused, identifying specific company practices rather than general calls for preventing social injustice. Non-governmental organisations (NGOs) are active in organizing boycotts, as are numerous other groups, ranging from animal rights and environmental campaigners to Islamic activists and minority groups (such as the Kurds of the Near East, the Ogoni of Nigeria, and the Karen of Myanmar). In the eyes of the organizers, boycotting is an attractive tool for "punishing" a target, achieving changes to the policies of a firm or government, and for rallying supporters.

Shell, the oil company, has been the target of numerous boycotts over the years, and is now prominent in its efforts to promote an image of corporate responsibility – as well as in practicing what it preaches. Its 2001 annual report makes extraordinary reading, with long sections on its policies on human rights, environmentalism, anti-terrorism, ethics, bribery, sustainable development, relations with governments, gender issues, its commitment to various NGO guidelines, and so on. The company's willingness to play ball with pressure groups has arguably led it to make some questionable decisions, such as the dismantling of the Brent Spar oil platform on land following widely-publicized activism. The platform, a concrete and steel structure used for oil storage, was decommissioned in 1991, and Shell had decided to sink it at sea, but Greenpeace campaigners boarded it in 1995, setting off an international boycott that cost Shell millions – one Shell station in

Germany was even firebombed. Shell's position was that it was safer and less expensive to scrap the platform at sea rather than doing so on land, a view supported by the British government. Greenpeace's initial claims that there were large amounts of oil left aboard the platform were shown to be untrue, as the group later accepted. The platform has now been towed to a Norwegian fiord, where it remains while Shell invites proposals for the most environmentally acceptable solution to the problem.

For marketers, naturally, boycotts are a nightmare. At the time of writing, there are more than 20 corporate boycotts underway in the UK alone, including: Air France, Unilever, Texaco, Suzuki, Reckitt & Colman, P&G, Philip Morris, Nike, Nestlé, L'Oreal, GAP, Esso, Dior, Colgate-Palmolive, Budweiser, and Bacardi.

Malicious rumors that won't die – the P&G logo

In the early 1980s P&G was suddenly faced with tens of thousands of calls from consumers demanding to know if it was true that the company's president was a satanist and if P&G's famous man-in-the-moon and stars logo was in fact a satanic symbol. Undoubtedly preposterous, you might think that this is the kind of rumor that a large firm can afford to ignore – but after 20 years, 250,000 phone calls, and 15 lawsuits, P&G still can't kill the story.

P&G first used its moon-and-stars logo in the 1850s as a trademark for its Star candles brand, when variations of the design were fashionable in the US. The firm's founders, incidentally, were practicing Christians. According to the rumors, however, P&G's president has appeared on a television talk-show to announce that he was a devil-worshipper, that P&G contributes large sums of money to the Church of Satan, and that this information can now be made public because there are too few Christians left in the US for the revelation to matter.

Variations of the rumor have been circulated periodically by leaflets, letters, e-mail and phone calls, usually with a list of P&G's key brands. P&G has obtained public condemnations of the story from Christian leaders of almost every denomination, as well as denials of the story from various talk-show hosts, including Phil Donohue, Jenny Jones, and Sally Jesse Raphael, all of whom were named at various times as the interviewer in the story.

So why won't the story go away? Part of the answer seems to lie in the competition between P&G and Amway, the network marketing firm. Although Amway is only about 15% of the size of P&G in terms of turnover, there is fierce rivalry between the two firms in the newly-opened markets of Asia, where evangelical Christian groups are mushrooming and there is widespread belief in the occult.

When the rumor first started, P&G discovered that some Amway representatives in the US were repeating the story to their colleagues and customers. After initiating lawsuits, P&G quickly obtained a promise from Amway to use its best efforts to stop its representatives spreading the rumor. According to an Amway lawyer, Charles Babcock, "we've bent over backwards to help Procter & Gamble stop this rumor."

One problem is that Amway, as a network marketing scheme, does not employ its "distributors," many of whom have little experience of business and earn, on average, very small sums from what they sell (distributor turnover is said to be as high as 50% annually). The firm may have little control over what their more naïve distributors tell potential customers – and, as a sales approach, the satanism story may be effective with certain customer groups.

In 1995, however, one of Amway's top salesmen, Randy Haugen, forwarded a version of the rumor on AmVox, a telephone messaging system for Amway distributors, which may have reached tens of thousands of distributors. Haugen quickly issued retractions – it appears that Haugen did not know that the rumor was false when he placed his message on AmVox. P&G sued, and in court Haugen testified that "I made a mistake. I wish I could retract it. I wish I had never done it."

Haugen's AmVox message was as follows:

"I wanna run something by you real quick that I think you will find pretty interesting. Just talking to a guy the other night about this very subject and it just so happens that a guy brings information in and lays it on my desk this morning, so here it goes."

"It says the president of Procter & Gamble appeared on the Phil Donohue Show on March 1, '95. He announced that due to the openness of our society, he was coming out of the closet about his association with the church of satan. He stated that a large portion of the profits from [P&G] products go to support his satanic church. When asked by Donohue if stating this on television would hurt his business, his reply was, 'There are not enough Christians in the United States to make a difference.' And below it has a list of the [P&G] products which I'll read: [the subject message then lists 43 P&G products].''

"It says if you are not sure about a product, look for the symbol of the ram's horn that will appear on each product beginning in April. The ram's horn will form the 666 which is known as Satan's number. I'll tell you it really makes you count your blessings to have available to all of us a business that allows us to buy all the products that we want from our own shelf and I guess my real question is, if people aren't being loyal to themselves and buying from their own business, then whose business are they supporting and who are they buying from. Love you. Talk to you later. Bye.''

P&G claims that it lost $49.5mn in sales of Tide, Crest, and Pampers between March 1995 and August 1997 because of the rumor. The lawsuits rumble on, and there is little sign that P&G will be able to scotch the allegations permanently.

Managing boycotts

For major firms, boycotts have become a fact of life and must be managed, both to limit the damage done and to try to avoid becoming a target in the first place. While some boycotts may lead to useful and legitimate reforms of company policy - few people can really feel that co-operating with foreign governments in murder is desirable, for instance - many are ethically ambiguous or have confused aims.

As we have seen, Shell is a leader in conducting "social" audits in an attempt to make its activities transparent and publicly acceptable. By holding dialogs with "stakeholders" and special interest groups, firms can, at the very least, identify problems that could lead to boycotts and take action ahead of time. By analyzing the ideological consensus in their key markets and conforming to it, firms can go a long way towards reducing the dangers of a well-organized, damaging boycott.

Another approach to damage limitation is to work to increase the strength of brands and the value given to customers. Consumers who set great store by a product have something to lose if they join in a boycott, and various studies suggest that this can significantly reduce the numbers of people who actually participate, even if they broadly approve of the reasons for the boycott. Good customer relations, and providing means for customers to express their views directly to the firm, may also do much to take the sting out of boycotts by giving people an alternative way of expressing their feelings.

But what should managers do once a boycott is underway? Here are some possible approaches.

» Few consumers hear about boycotts when they are first called, so firms do not need to respond immediately. It is important, however, to monitor the progress of the boycott to see if it is gaining momentum, and also, perhaps, to make changes in the practice that is being attacked. Often, boycotts get big after media exposure, so rehearsing the arguments carefully in preparation for journalists' questions may limit the damage. It is much easier to sensationalize an issue if the management refuses to talk, or behaves in a way that appears shifty. Showing the media that the firm understands the issues and is taking a well thought-out, defensible position may do much to divert attention elsewhere.

» As marketers of sweets, cream cakes, and ice cream know, advertising campaigns aimed at making consumers feel less guilty about buying a product can be effective. Although the fear of getting fat may be different from, say, feeling guilty about purchasing your favorite brand because you are not showing solidarity with a boycott, guilt-assuaging campaigns may reduce the number of people who feel obliged to join a boycott by providing them with arguments for continuing to purchase.

» When firms have to recall products, they generally reduce their advertising for a while. Some may do the same during a boycott, but it may be smarter to increase advertising because it reminds boycotters of what they are giving up.

» Set up customer information lines to field boycott-related complaints and produce literature setting out the firm's position.

KEY LEARNING POINTS

» The number of consumer boycotts is increasing, and many are organized by NGOs. In the past, firms often dismissed such actions as emanating from a lunatic fringe, but suffered when the boycotts became widespread (such as the Saran Wrap boycott during the Vietnam War).

» Today, progressive firms try to align themselves with the public consensus in their major markets. Green issues and ideas about healthy living, for example, are now mainstream in the West, and firms such as Shell go out of their way to both behave in ways that are seen as responsible and to publicize the fact.

» Not all attacks on firms are justifiable – the P&G ''satanism'' rumor being an obvious example – but still have an effect. Firms must accept that they may not be able to kill an issue altogether, but can mitigate the damage by running an ongoing effort to inform the public of the facts and, where necessary, sue for libel.

» Giving consumers the means to vent their anger, such as providing information lines and setting up meetings with stakeholder groups, may help to find a satisfactory resolution. The issues are often more complex than the boycotters initially suggest – for instance, in the case of Brent Spar, it is not at all clear what the most environmentally responsible action would have been.

Resources

- » Books.
- » Websites.
- » Further reading.

BOOKS

For God, Country and Coca-Cola, Mark Pendergrast (Scribner, 1993)

This detailed history of the rise of Coca-Cola provides one of the most useful insights into how FMCG marketing developed. Although the book is billed as "unauthorized," Pendergrast seems to have obtained extensive access to company files and is broadly sympathetic to the firm. Coke's failures are examined, such as the attempt to change the formula in the 1980s, as are its successes, such as its ability to continue to expand in the face of serious opposition from activists of all kinds.

Throughout its life, Coke has been dominated by a few strong leaders. Robert Woodruff, who took over in 1919, was a tough Southern businessman who built the brand's strength in the US over many decades, while a successor, the Cuban Roberto Goizueta, presided over Coke's expansion overseas until his untimely death in 1997. Coke has also had its share of melodrama and shady political deals, both at home and abroad. The legend of Coke's secret formula is typical of the company's brilliance at public relations – in fact, there's no big secret about the recipe, and the value of the product lies in the brand, not the flavor (a competitor cannot market a rival cola as "Coca-Cola"). Woodruff promoted the story of the secret formula, making a big show of keeping the only written copy of the recipe in a safe-deposit box at his bank, and even today, the company claims that only two executives know the mysteries of Coke's ingredients and their proportions.

Although it is unlikely that a new firm could imitate Coke's extraordinary success, there is much to learn from this long-lived giant. Unusually concentrated ownership and bosses with a very long tenure have enabled the company to pursue its policies consistently until they have produced results – evidence that powerful leadership may be better for firms in the long term than the incessant pursuit of the latest marketing fashions.

No Logo: Taking Aim at the Brand Bullies, Naomi Klein (Flamingo, 2001)

Love it or hate it, this polemical tome has become the bible for the anti-multinational movement, and no one concerned with selling to consumers can afford to ignore it. The author, Naomi Klein, is a young Canadian activist who attacks branding and its role in the rise of globalization. While some of its arguments are wildly off the mark, or just plain wrong, such as the idea that corporate foreign direct investment necessarily leads to job losses and economic troubles at home, her criticisms of brands touch a nerve. Although the book inaccurately portrays brands as becoming ever-more powerful, it actually helps to explain why consumers are becoming less brand-loyal.

Privately, even many people in the consumer product business are sick of brands and brand advertising. As early as 1963, David Ogilvy, the founder of the Ogilvy & Mather advertising agency, wrote: "When I retire from Madison Avenue, I am going to start a secret society of masked vigilantes who will travel around the world on silent motor bicycles, chopping down posters at the dark of the moon" (*Confessions of an Advertising Man*). Klein charts the process where, since the 1980s, many brand manufacturers have evolved away from making their goods to becoming almost purely marketing firms, and have managed to associate brands with many icons of rebellion and counter-culture, from the Rolling Stones to gay activism. The anodyne ubiquity of shopping malls, harsh conditions for factory workers in developing countries, the anatomy of anti-capitalist activism, and the use of corporate power in the media are all covered, albeit in a tediously one-sided way.

Ms Klein doesn't appear to understand much about business, but that's not why the book is important. FMCG companies have to realize – and many do – just how many consumers have a schizophrenic attitude, detesting their marketing methods while still purchasing the goods. Today, the real challenge is in understanding the reasons for this and evolving selling approaches that are acceptable. Companies that get this right are likely to be rewarded very richly indeed.

Store Wars: The Battle for Mindspace and Shelfspace, Judith and Marcel Corstjens (Wiley, 1999)

FMCG selling today is primarily focused on the battle for power between the retailers and their major suppliers. Food prices have been relatively low for years, and competition on price is all-important, which favors the larger players. *Store Wars* is a serious study of the issues, examining the various ploys that large firms use to get ahead and looking at the phenomenon of co-operation between rivals. Retailers now have the upper hand, but are not all the same. For example, although the chains Aldi and Tesco have roughly the same turnover, Aldi has a larger number of small stores with a limited range of products. Aldi enjoys greater economies of scale in its purchasing power but Tesco, with its bigger stores, saves money on its outlets. This useful book has a large number of case studies that illustrate the problems – and some solutions – in the FMCG jungle.

WEBSITES

Link and portal sites

Zenith Media

http://www.zenithmedia.com/
Media services agency Zenith Media was formed in 1995 as a merger of the media service units of Saatchi & Saatchi and Bates. Clients include many of the big names in FMCG. The site is a ''marketers' portal,'' providing a very wide range of links, many of which are relevant to FMCG.

FMCG Net

http://murals.users.netlink.co.uk/fmcgnet.html
Links to many of the major premium-brand sites, from Ben & Jerry's ice cream to Snickers chocolate, the major advertising agencies, marketing journals, and market research companies.

Food Manufacturing Forum

http://www.mts.net/~ccooke/food/Press.html
The site doesn't seem to be regularly updated, but provides useful information and links of interest to small food manufacturers.

Regulators

Food and Drug Administration (FDA)

http://www.fda.gov/
The FDA is America's regulator. Superbly informative, like so many US government sites, there is detailed and accurate information on

a very wide range of issues, from GM foods and nut allergies to the full publication of the Federal codes affecting food and drink. Vast, user-friendly, and intelligent.

Food Standards Agency

http://www.foodstandards.gov.uk/
Less comprehensive and much more "dumbed down" than the FDA site, the UK's regulator, the Food Standards Agency, provides useful information on domestic food issues, including news of EU regulations.

Research organizations and consultancies

ACNielsen

http://www.acnielsen.com/
One of the largest research groups, ACNielsen's site contains many press releases relating to the company's activities around the world. Some of these may be of news interest – for example, at the time of writing it reports that one of its US surveys found that Hispanic households in Los Angeles are much less likely to belong to a grocery store frequent-shopper program than non-Hispanics. The really useful data, of course, is not free.

NPD Group

http://www.npd.com/
NPD Group serves the major manufacturers and retailers with market information in many industries, including FMCG. Clients include Unilever and many retailers worldwide. Provides point-of-sale tracking data.

Professional Assignments Group (PAG)

http://www.pag.com/
Quirky Australian grocery consultancy PAG is focused on providing support services for salespeople in the industry, particularly in relation to trade spend and trade marketing. It has a proprietary software system for managing trade spend that has been bought by Nestlé Australia, Heinz, Johnson Wax, Cadbury New Zealand, and others. PAG offers training at all levels, from basic sales to account management.

The site is of interest to people working in other parts of the world because of its highly detailed articles on category management, trade promotion, and so on.

Academic

Aspects of FMCG are widely studied by scholars, and there is a great wealth of material available online. The problem for the practitioner is in finding material that is directly relevant and applicable in business. As an example of academic research that is genuinely useful, if heavy-going, try: http://www.marketing.wharton.upenn.edu/people/faculty/bell.html.

David R. Bell is Associate Professor of Marketing, University of Pennsylvania. His interests include consumer choice, price-setting and contracts, and arrangements in channels of distribution. He is currently studying the effect of consumer research and information provision on prices posted and paid. Relevant papers available online include the following.

» "Seven Barriers to Customer Equity Management," with J. Deighton, W.J. Reinartz, R. Rust, and G. Schwartz. Forthcoming in *Journal of Services Research.*
» "Creating Win-Win Trade Promotions: Theory and Empirical Analysis of Scan-Back Trade Deals," with Xavier Drèze. Forthcoming in *Marketing Science* (2003).
» "The Inter-Store Mobility of Supermarket Shoppers," with Hongjai Rhee. Forthcoming in *Journal of Retailing.*
» "An Experimental and Empirical Analysis of Consumer Response to Stockouts," with G. J. Fitzsimons.
» "Coupon Bundles and Consumer Budgets," with J. Chiang. Revising for second review in *Marketing Science.*
» "Changing the Channel: A Better Way to Do Trade Promotions," with Xavier Drèze. *Sloan Management Review*, 43(2), pp. 42-50.
» "Store Choice and Shopping Behavior: How Price Format Works," with C.S. Tang and Teck-Hua Ho. *California Management Review*, 43 (2) (Winter), pp. 54-74.
» "Looking for Loss Aversion in Scanner Panel Data: The Confounding Effect of Price Response Heterogeneity," with J. M. Lattin. *Marketing Science* (2000), 19(2), pp. 185-200.

» "Shopping Behavior and Consumer Preference for Store Price Format: Why 'Large Basket' Shoppers Prefer EDLP," with J.M. Lattin. *Marketing Science* (1990), **17**(1), pp. 66–88.

Conferences

Institute of Grocery Distribution (IGD)

http://www.igd.org.uk/

IGD's site lists its conferences, including the UK's Food Industry Awards, and provides some research and analysis of individual retailers.

Wal-Mart

http://www.walmartstores.com

Wal-Mart has a reputation for fair dealing with its suppliers, and provides useful information on its Website about how to become one, with its "Supplier Proposal Packet," which includes a questionnaire list of requirements, procedural outline, and so on. It also provides details of its vendor standards.

Key account managers

KAM City

http://www.kamcity.com/navtext/

This Website is designed for FMCG key account managers, and has a wealth of useful material, including addresses and links of major retailers and manufacturers around the world, training information, KAM news, books, and trade shows.

Articles

Ernst & Young

http://www.ey.com

Ernst & Young has a number of useful articles on FMCG issues available in PDF format.

Newsgroups

Anarchic discussion fora. Some are for amateurs, some for professionals, and some are mixed – can be a good source of insight into what consumers are thinking.

alt.food
alt.food.cocacola
alt.food.coffee
alt.food.fat-free
alt.food.pancakes
alt.food.sushi
alt.food.wine
alt.creative-cook
alt.coffee
alt.cereal
alt.creative-cooking
alt.drinks.kool-aid
alt.mcdonalds
ba.food (San Francisco Bay Area food)
bionet.molbio.ageing (diet & aging)
rec.food.chocolate
rec.food.cooking
rec.food.drink
rec.food.drink.beer
rec.food.drink.coffee
rec.food.drink.tea
rec.food.historic
rec.food.preserving
rec.food.recipes
rec.food.restaurants
rec.food.sourdough
rec.food.veg
sci.bio.food-science
sci.bio.technology
sci.med.nutrition

FURTHER READING

» Bernheim, B. Douglas & Whinston, Michael D. (1990) "Multimarket
  Contact and Collusive Behavior." *RAND Journal of Economics*,
  21(1), pp. 1–26.

» Borden, N. (1942) *The Economic Effects of Advertising*. Richard D. Irwin, Chicago.

» Braithwaite, D. (1928) "The Economic Effects of Advertising," *Economic Journal*, **38**, 16–37.

» Cannondale Associates, Inc. (2001) "Bridging the Gap, Category/Loyalty Management Survey." Wilton, CT.

» Chevalier, Judy K., Kashyap, Anil K., & Rossi, Peter E. (2000) "Why Don't Prices Rise During Periods of Peak Demand? Evidence from Scanner Data." National Bureau of Economic Research Working Paper 7981, October.

» Cook, V.J. & Schutte, T.F. (1967) *Brand Policy Determination*. Marketing Science Institute, Boston, Allyn & Bacon.

» Cotterill, R.W. & Putsis, W.P., Jr (2000) "Market Share and Price Setting Behavior for Private Labels and National Brands." *Review of Industrial Organization*, **17**, pp. 19–39.

» Dhar, S.K. & Hoch, S.J. (1997) "Why Store Brand Penetration Varies by Retailer." *Marketing Science*, **16**, pp. 208–227.

» Drèze, X., Hoch, S.J., & Purk, M.E. (1994) "Shelf Management and Space Elasticity," *Journal of Retailing*, **70**, pp. 301–326.

» Fogg-Meade, E. (1901) "The Place of Advertising in Modern Business." *Journal of Political Economy*, **9**, pp. 218–242.

» Hoch, S.J. & Banerji, S. (1993) "When do Private Labels Succeed?," *Sloan Management Review*, **34**, pp. 57–67.

» Hoch, S.J. & Lodish, L.M. (1998) "Store Brands and Category Management." Working Paper, The Wharton School, University of Pennsylvania, Philadelphia, PA.

» Hoch, S.J., Montgomery, A.L., & Park, Y.-H. (2002) "Why the Private Label is one of the Few Brands to Show Consistent Long Term." Paper presented at Allied Social Sciences Association annual meeting, Atlanta, Georgia, January 5, 2000.

» KPMG (1999) "Customer Loyalty and Private Label Products." KPMG Global Consumer Markets.

» Hosken, D. & Reiffen, D. (2001) "How Do Retailers Determine Sale Products: Evidence from Store-level Data." Federal Trade Commission, Working Paper, June 2001.

» Lal, Rajiv & Matutes, Carmen (1994) "Retail Pricing and Advertising Strategies." *Journal of Business*, **67**, pp. 345-70.
» Lal, Rajiv & Villas-Boas, J. Miguel (1998) "Price Promotions and Trade Deals with Multiproduct Retailers." *Management Science*, **44**, pp. 935-949.
» MacDonald, James M. (2000) "Demand, Information and Competition: Why Do Food Prices Fall at Seasonal Demand Peaks?" *The Journal of Industrial Economics*, **48**(1), pp. 27-45.
» Morton, F.S. & Zettelmeyer, F. (2000) "The Strategic Positioning of Store Brands in Retailer–Manufacturer Bargaining." Unpublished paper presented at FTC, Bureau of Economics, September 28.
» McKinsey & Co. (1972) "Private Label Survey." New York.
» Narasimhan, C. & Wilcox, R.T. (1998) "Private Labels and the Channel Relationship: A Cross-Category Analysis." *Journal of Business*, **71**, pp. 573-600.
» Nolan, P., (1999) "Coca-Cola and the global business revolution: a study with special reference to the EU." University of Cambridge, Judge Institute of Management Studies.
» Pendergrast, Mark (1993) *For God, Country and Coca-Cola*. Charles Scribner & Sons, New York.
» Pesendorfer, Martin, (1998) "Retail Sales: A Study of Pricing Behavior in Supermarkets." Working paper, Yale University.
» Rodmell, P. (20001) "Refining Retail Brand Strategies." *DSN Retailing Today*, **48**, p. 11.
» Rotemberg, Julio J. & Saloner, Garth (1986) "A Super-game Theoretic Model of Business Cycles and Price Wars During Booms." *American Economic Review*, **76**(3), pp. 390-407.
» Rotemberg, Julio J. & Woodford, Michael (1991) "Mark-ups and the Business Cycle." *Macroeconomics Annual*, **6**, pp. 63-129.
» Sethuraman, R. (1996) "A Model of How Discounting High-Priced Brands Affects the Sales of Low-Priced Brands." *Journal of Marketing Research*, **33**, pp. 399-409.
» Sethuraman, R. (2000) "What Makes Consumers Pay More for National Brands Than for Store Brands: Image or Quality?" MSI Working Paper, Report No. 99-110.
» Setlow, C. (1998) "Roper on Retail," *Discount Store·News*, p. 37.

» Sharp, Gene (1973) *The Politics of Non-violent Action*. Porter Sargent, Boston.

» Shell (1998) *Profits and Principles – does there have to be a choice?* Shell International, London.

» Shell (2001) *People, Planet and Profits: The Shell Report*. Shell International, London.

» Sivakumar K. & Raj, S.P. (1997) "Quality Tier Competition: How Price Change Influences Brand Choice." *Journal of Marketing*, **61**, pp. 71-84.

» Steiner, R.L. (1991) "Intrabrand Competition - Stepchild of Antitrust." *Antitrust Bulletin*, **36**, pp. 155-200.

» Steiner, R.L. (1993) "The Inverse Association Between the Margins of Manufacturers and Retailers." *Review of Industrial Organization*, **8**, pp. 717-740.

» Steiner, R.L. (2000) "The Third Relevant Market." *Antitrust Bulletin*, **45**, pp. 719-759.

» Steiner, R. L. (1973) "Does Advertising Lower Consumer Prices?" *Journal of Marketing*, **37**, pp. 19-26.

» Simester, Duncan (1995) "Signaling Price Image Using Advertised Prices." *Marketing Science*, **14**(n.2), pp. 166-188.

» Warner, Elizabeth J. & Barsky, Robert B. (1995) "The Timing and Magnitude of Retail Store Markdowns: Evidence from Weekends and Holiday." *Quarterly Journal of Economics*, **110**, pp. 321-52.

Ten Steps to Making FMCG Selling Work

Key opportunities and issues in FMCG selling, including:

» innovation;
» don't fool yourself with the data;
» private labels;
» can retailers really go global?;
» are brands still in crisis?;
» shelf management;
» trade promotions;
» slotting fees;
» boycotts; and
» RFID tags.

1. INNOVATION

FMCG firms were among the great innovators in mass-marketing techniques. P&G, founded in 1837, invented or developed many of the methods that are now the mainstay of consumer marketing, most notably brand management and product differentiation, which it adopted in the late 1930s. It also pioneered research into consumer behavior, and went to extraordinary lengths to discover how its customers really used their products, and what improvements they wanted.

Once regarded as the great innovator, P&G has become less inventive in recent years, despite the occasional success, such as Always, the sanitary pad with "wings," and "Sunny Delight," an orange-flavored drink. Currently it is attempting to reform itself to make it easier for new products to reach the market faster. The increasing power of retailers poses a threat to manufacturers, particularly through their own brands, but so far they have generally been imitations of leading brands rather than innovative products.

With the enormous difficulty of successfully introducing a new item, many people shy away from them altogether, arguing that the risks are too great. One notable exception, however, is the Red Bull energy drink, that single-handedly created a new category and reached its well-targeted market through non-conventional means. Red Bull's founder knew exactly what he was doing – this was not a case of luck, but of superb marketing by a seasoned professional.

2. DON'T FOOL YOURSELF WITH THE DATA

Scanner data, the foundation of category management, can be a two-edged sword. On the one hand, it promises the potential to target consumers much more precisely and to make the whole supply-chain much more efficient. On the other, the extraordinarily large amount of data can confuse non-experts and lead to bad decisions.

One poor practice that is widespread is to rank brand sales figures across regions or a whole chain. This is a very blunt tool, given the wide variation in consumer behavior at individual stores, and is very unlikely to optimize the product mix within categories.

There are also problems with the industry-wide data supplied by research firms. While these firms do their best to ensure accuracy, there is evidence that some of the figures are massaged by the companies that supply them. Making decisions based on other people's bad data is clearly less than ideal.

Using scanner data favors the largest firms, who have the capital to invest in state-of-the-art hardware that can handle it. The promise of extremely accurate marketing targeted at individual stores and, perhaps, ultimately at individual consumers, is not really within reach for the smaller players.

3. PRIVATE LABELS

As a competitive strategy, the retailers' entry into producing their own private label brands is little short of masterful – since they control the shelves, why shouldn't they make some of what is sold on them? Consumer acceptance of private labels is increasing, particularly in countries where the market is dominated by a handful of large chains. Once they discover a private label that is "as good as" the premium brand, the customer seems happy to buy it, particularly since it is likely to be cheaper.

For the retailer, private labels are more profitable, and give greater flexibility in pricing decisions. They also reduce the risk of losing out from the "free rider" effect, where a retailer helps to build a manufacturer's brand and then finds that competitors begin to stock it.

So far, retailers have generally shied away from product innovation, which may give the large manufacturers a fighting chance. Retailers still need the premium brands in order to get customers to come into their stores. For manufacturers with weaker, second- or third-tier brands, the future looks bleak as they are being squeezed out of the market. For premium brands, however, price is still a weapon against private labels, since studies show that a price cut in a premium brand hurts private labels much more than a private label price-cut hurts the leading brand.

4. CAN RETAILERS REALLY GO GLOBAL?

Supermarket chains are still at a very early stage of going global, and there are still worries that they will not be able to make consistent long-term profits in foreign markets. In spite of their expertise and buying power, many analysts feel that they are failing to adapt sensitively to local customers, especially in the developing world. One chain, for example, was criticized in Brazil for badly organized parking which did not take into account that customers tend to come for major shopping trips at the weekend.

Perhaps it is a sign that globalization is not all it should be that the country that most frequently internationalizes its businesses, the US, has been very slow to do so in retailing. The much-touted foreign expansion of Wal-Mart is the only exception, and there are doubts about its effectiveness.

While European retailers have to consolidate within the EU as much as possible in order to survive, the strategy behind their expansion in other parts of the world is less clear. The huge distances involved make many economies of scale impossible, and until they attain a substantial size globally, they will be unable to negotiate prices on a global basis with the leading brands.

So far, it has been about doing the retailing job better than smaller, less sophisticated local firms, but as Royal Ahold's experience in Shanghai shows, local stores may be quick to learn their lessons and ultimately squeeze the foreigners out.

5. ARE BRANDS STILL IN CRISIS?

In some respects, the art of branding is a victim of its own success. When brands became tradable during the financial deregulation of the 1980s, many people became very excited about brands without really understanding what they are. Successful brands, old and new, are lovingly cultivated over many years by committed marketing teams that stay as close as possible to the consumer's needs and attitudes. Merely printing logos does not constitute branding, and the whole concept has been talked to death.

Meanwhile, however, many of the best brands maintain their lead, in part by avoiding unwinnable wars – for example, cigarette manufacturers are not going to make a lot of headway in the health-conscious West.

Part of the secret in brand-building seems to be in stability over the long term. It's the commitment of owners and managers to make the brand the very best of its type and keep it that way that lies at the core of true "brand equity." Imitations, lookalikes, and half-hearted publicity ploys are unlikely to win the permanent goodwill of their customers, and serve to "commoditize" brands, which is the opposite of the desired result.

6. SHELF MANAGEMENT

Although there is much more research to be done in this field, there is evidence that many retail chains could improve their returns by "micro-managing" the shelf space in individual stores. The problem is that, with so many categories and product items, retailers do not have enough staff to micro-manage everything. Even picking a few key categories, however, could yield substantial benefits in terms of increased profits.

Manufacturers seem to be right in attaching so much importance to good shelf positions, even though they disagree somewhat in what the ideal position should be. According to the study discussed in Chapter 6 ("Managing shelf space better"), the best positions are at "eye level," meaning slightly below the average horizontal view, at 51-53 inches off the floor. The vertical position – how near it is to eye level – seems to be much more important than the horizontal position.

Another important finding for manufacturers is that the amount of shelf space – the "facing" – is less important than is generally thought. Above a certain size, which varies from category to category, getting extra facing has no effect on sales whatsoever.

7. TRADE PROMOTIONS

Manufacturers in the US say that only 16% of trade promotions are profitable for them, yet because of the competitive nature of the industry they are forced to keep using them extensively. Retailers think they are wasteful too, but tend to support them because they are a useful source of extra profits.

Most trade promotions are off-invoice, which means that retailers get the extra discount on any amount of the product they purchase during the promotion period. This produces a gaping loophole which many of them exploit, first by "diverting," which means buying more product than they need and selling the excess to other retailers at slightly higher than the promotional discount price, and second, by buying excess promotional product and selling it later at full price, or continuing to run the promotion after it is supposed to have finished. One leading brand manufacturer found that a store sold 335% more product during a year than it actually ordered, presumably because it was purchasing from another retailer who was "diverting."

Scanner data ought to be a way for manufacturers to control these ploys, but since retailers control the data, they need to be persuaded. Why should a retailer co-operate? Perhaps the best way is to offer them a better deal, since pay-for-performance "scan-back" promotions prevent them from profiting by breaking the promotional agreement. If the deals are generous enough, trials have shown that it is possible to stabilize the purchase pattern of the retailer. Unstable demand due to diverting and other practices is one of the main reasons why manufacturers run promotions in the first place.

8. SLOTTING FEES

Some top manufacturers refuse to pay them, and some retailers, such as Wal-Mart, prefer more scientific approaches, but the practice of charging slotting allowances is widespread. Although manufacturers feel that paying these fees does not guarantee better sales, the evidence that certain shelf positions really do have a markedly powerful effect on sales means that they may be justified in some instances.

These fees are a symptom of the growth in retailer power, but they indicate huge inefficiency in the industry. Wal-Mart's category management approach, providing a large amount of accurate data to suppliers so that they can plan their activities effectively, may be better – as the world's largest retailer, Wal-Mart's views certainly carry some credibility.

9. BOYCOTTS

No Logo author, Naomi Klein, struck a chord when she described brand marketing as creating "a Barbie world for adults." Many consumers in the West are becoming increasingly active in product boycotts and other actions intended to foster social justice and other reforms. The radical politics of the 1960s have become today's dreary truisms as that generation has attained political power.

Firms have to take such activities seriously, but they need not feel unduly threatened. Promoting an image of corporate responsibility, instituting reasonable changes, entering into dialog with lobby groups, and generally trying to align themselves with the public consensus in their markets is frequently effective. Taking a combative position is probably unwise, given the power of the media, which has an incentive to dramatize and promote the boycotters' viewpoints.

10. RFID TAGS

If you thought scanner data was already hard for the industry to digest, think what may happen if RFID tags, little radio-activated memory chips that contain scanner data, are introduced. If they become cheap enough, it will be possible to monitor closely the progress of individual items through the whole supply chain and, ultimately, into the home of the consumer.

The information that RFIDs could generate would swamp the vast, unmanageable quantities already available, but could take some power away from retailers, since others may be able to capture the data too. More importantly, once methods have been found to process the information effectively, marketing may become more powerful and efficient than ever before.

KEY LEARNING POINTS

» There are too many new products chasing too little space in the stores, and the majority of launches fail. Success may depend on finding a new market segment and unconventional ways of reaching it.

» We hear a lot about the incredible potential of scanner data in focused marketing, but the reality is that only the biggest stores have the infrastructure to manage it properly. Shared data across the industry is widely regarded as tainted due to misreporting, and without proper training managers are likely to misinterpret it. Be careful!

» Private labels are more profitable for retailers than other brands, and are being used to drive out the second- and third-tier products.

» The jury is still out on whether retailers can successfully internationalize. We won't know for sure for some years to come.

» "True" brands are built from the bottom up and take years to reach maturity. There is no quick route to creating a really solid brand, as many dot.com companies found out during the dot.com bust.

» Eye-level shelf space is almost certainly the best position for most products. Horizontal position is much less important.

» Pay-for-performance promotions are a way of trying to prevent retailers from "cheating" in promotions. To persuade retailers to accept them, manufacturers need to be generous.

» Slotting fees are often seen as a kind of blackmail. They are certainly a sign of inefficiency. Properly run category management schemes have no need for these kinds of fees, since all the partners in the supply chain work together to optimize sales.

» Firms can no longer afford to ignore consumer activism. Most boycotts start small and have little effect in the beginning, but firms need to monitor their progress, since when they become widely known the effects on sales can be devastating.

» Radio frequency identification, or RFID, uses small memory chips ("tags") with a tiny radio antenna to transmit data about the object to which it is attached. Wal-Mart is investing heavily in them as a way of making supply chain management more efficient, and in the future they may open the way to new, very potent, marketing methods.

Frequently Asked Questions (FAQs)

Q1: What is category management?

A: See Chapter 2, "Category management."

Q2: What are the origins of market research?

A: See Chapter 3, "Procter & Gamble – the great innovator."

Q3: What's wrong with brand-ranking as a way of deciding what products to stock?

A: See Chapter 4, "The challenge of 'data mining'."

Q4: What is an SKU?

A: See Chapter 2, "Slotting allowances and other payments."

Q5: What is RFID?

A: See Chapter 4, "Coming soon – RFID tags."

Q6: Why might the Euro drive down prices of FMCG?

A: See Chapter 5, "Is the Euro deflationary for FMCG?"

Q7: Why do manufacturers run trade promotions when they are unprofitable?

A: See Chapter 6, "The trouble with trade promotions."

Q8: Why do many retailers dislike providing scanner data to their major suppliers?

A: See Chapter 6, "The trouble with trade promotions."

Q9: Is it still possible for a new company to launch a new FMCG product successfully?

A: See Chapter 7, "The Red Bull generation."

Q10: Does Coca-Cola actually make Coca-Cola?

A: See Chapter 7, "Carbonated soft drinks (CSD) in the US – Coke and Pepsi."

Index

EXPRESSEXEC –
BUSINESS THINKING AT YOUR FINGERTIPS

ExpressExec is a 12-module resource with 10 titles in each module. Combined they form a complete resource of current business practice. Each title enables the reader to quickly understand the key concepts and models driving management thinking today.

Available from:
www.expressexec.com

Customer Service Department
John Wiley & Sons Ltd
Southern Cross Trading Estate
1 Oldlands Way, Bognor Regis
West Sussex, PO22 9SA
Tel: +44(0)1243 843 294
Fax: +44(0)1243 843 303
Email: cs-books@wiley.co.uk